PUBLIC LANDS, PUBLIC DEBATES

Public Lands, Public Debates

A CENTURY OF CONTROVERSY

Char Miller

Oregon State University Press
Corvallis

The paper in this book meets the guidelines for permanence and durability of the Committee on Production Guidelines for Book Longevity of the Council on Library Resources and the minimum requirements of the American National Standard for Permanence of Paper for Printed Library Materials Z39.48-1984.

Library of Congress Cataloging-in-Publication Data
Miller, Char, 1951-
  Public lands, public debates : a century of controversy / Char Miller.
    p. cm.
  Includes index.
  ISBN 978-0-87071-659-1 (pbk. : alk. paper)
  -- ISBN 978-0-87071-660-7 (e-book)
  1. Forest reserves--United States--Management. 2. Public lands--United States--Management. 3. United States. Forest Service. 4. United States. Bureau of Land Management. I. Title.
  SD426.M54 2012
  333.730973--dc23

                        2011053116

First published in 2012 by Oregon State University Press
Printed in the United States of America

Oregon State University Press
121 The Valley Library
Corvallis OR 97331-4501
541-737-3166 • fax 541-737-3170
http://osupress.oregonstate.edu

TABLE OF CONTENTS

ACKNOWLEDGEMENTS

I have been very lucky to work with a group of editors who have given me space in their pages to try out some of the arguments that weave throughout *Public Lands, Public Debates*. Better still, they did their readers a huge favor by slashing through my prose with red pen, or Track Changes; they tightened its claims, forced me to think more carefully about the words I had chosen to convey them, helping me to make my case better than I had done. Among others, I am particularly grateful to Zach Behrens, Robert Critchlow, James G. Lewis, Patricia Marshall, Shellie Nelson, Rebecca Staebler, Matthew Walls, and Elaine Wolff; and to the editorial and technical staff at (and, where relevant, their outside reviewers for) *Forest History Today, Headwaters.org, Journal of Forestry, Journal of Policy History, KCET: SoCal Focus, The Pinchot Letter, San Antonio Current, Society and Natural Resources*, and the University of Arizona Press. Special thanks to Martin Nie of the University of Montana; and V. Alaric Sample, President of the Pinchot Institute: they permitted me to revise our co-authored essays for republication in this context and have been stellar guides to the complex art of interpreting the forces that have shaped the history and present state of our public lands.

It has been my privilege as well to work with colleagues at Oregon State University Press. This is the fourth project on which we have collaborated, and I have been the decided beneficiary of the staff's keen insights and shrewd instincts, critical survival skills during this tough period in American publishing. As in the past, so with this book: Mary Braun, Jo Alexander, Micki Reaman, and Tom Booth have given it their all.

There are no words to thank my family, those learning to walk and those who no longer walk this earth, for their encouragement, love, and laughter. The same goes for my students at Trinity University and now Pomona College; they have pushed me to become a better teacher of their writing, which has helped with my own. I am honored to dedicate this book to them.

INTRODUCTION
In the Woods

In his foreword to Paul W. Gates' massive tome, *History of Public Land Law Development*, Rep. Wayne Aspinall, head of the Public Land Law Review Commission (1965-1970), for which the book had been written, was trying to be something that his many critics doubted he could ever be—-even handed. The Colorado Democrat offered this balancing caution to those ready to plunge into the 828-page document: "The members of the Commission probably will not unanimously agree with all the inferences and observations of the authors," Aspinall noted, and doubted that "all members of the Advisory Council and all of the Governors' Representatives will agree with the viewpoints expressed by the authors." Caveat lector.[1]

Aspinall was partly speaking about himself: as the long-serving chair of the House Interior and Insular Affairs Committee (1959-1973), he had been a canny and pugnacious opponent of many of that era's most significant pieces of environmental legislation affecting the nation's public lands; he wanted greater exploitation of their varied resources, water-development projects especially, and championed a much smaller federal regulatory footprint, which lead him to denounce the Wilderness Act and disdain endangered-species protections. As David Brower, then-executive director of the Sierra Club, famously declared: "dream after dream dashed on the stony continents of Wayne Aspinall."[2]

Whatever his individual animus, Aspinall's resistance was part of a larger cultural narrative, a pattern that Gates' thoroughly documented book confirms: Americans have always fought over the public lands, about their physical existence, political purposes, economic benefits, and environmental values. About them, we have never reached unanimous accord.

The battle over them began before there was such a thing as an "American," before there was an institutionalized concept of "public lands." Central to these early conflicts was the European powers' granting of lands to those founding colonial settlements in North America. In the case of Great Britain, Gates writes that its "extraordinarily liberal charters or grants to proprietors" established the thirteen colonies, whose boundaries "were ill-defined, overlapping, and crossed with Indian occupancy claims and trading rights." This set of initial complications only intensified, a result of each colony adopting its own system of distributing those acres under its control (and lots that were not). In hopes of clarifying these blurred lines of authority and power, England, following the 1763 Treaty of Paris, in which it gained control of most of the eastern half of North America, tried to impose its will on how colonial governors and legislatures distributed property. This imposition "irked influential people that an absentee government in which they were not represented could exercise such powers." One of them was Thomas Jefferson, who, in his 1774 brief, "Summary View of the Rights of British America," disputed the Mother Country's primacy. All "lands within which the limits of any particular society has circumscribed around itself, are assumed by that society, and subject to their allotment only," the magnate of Monticello asserted. The right to do so was lodged in the people's "sovereign authority," collectively proclaimed or legislatively declared; and if unstated, it devolved to the individual, who "may appropriate to himself such lands as he finds vacant, and occupancy will give him title." The war over the public domain was joined.[3]

The successful conclusion of the Revolutionary War, and land-claims settlements between states old and new, changed the context of that battle. Henceforth it would be, as Gates puts it, "thrashed out" between the states and central government. A thrashing it has been, too. Every permutation of that oft-pitched, two-century-long struggle to define the ownership and purposes of the public lands is deftly chronicled in Gates' thick text. The early-nineteenth-century brawls as each new state entered the union get full treatment: the distribution of the public domain in support of internal-improvement projects and public education, to promote settlement, and honor veterans as well as the successful memorial from reformer Dorothea Dix seeking the sale of five million acres to support the housing and care of the insane. The generous-to-a-fault railroad grants, and a raft of give-away measures disguised as reform legislation, including the Timber Culture Act (1877), Desert Land Act (1877), Timber and Stone Act (1878), also are thoroughly vetted. As are the Progressive Era measures that launched what would become the Forest Service and the national forest system and subsequently kicked off a storm of protest. With the public lands, there has never been a dull moment.

So it is something of a puzzle that Gates concluded his study on an optimistic note. Writing about the emergence of the various systems of federal management of the public lands from the vantage point of the late 1960s—hardly a quiet time—he argued that once-powerful sectional interests had lost their sway; that the greatest threat to these assets might come henceforth from those who loved them to death—hikers, campers, and other recreational users; and that there was a welcome tempering of the clash between those who favored strong federal control of these public assets and those Jeffersonians like Aspinall who felt the states should have greater control of these resources, if not outright sovereignty over them. "Many Americans take great pride in the national parks, enjoy the recreational facilities in the national forests, and in large numbers tour the giant dams and reservoirs of the Reclamation Service," Gates observed. "National pride in the possession and enjoyment of these facilities seems to be displacing earlier views."[4]

The tensions—regionally based and/or user driven—instead have continued unabated. This has been true of each new session of Congress, regardless of which political party holds power in which branch, and notwithstanding whether a Democrat or Republican occupies the White House. They appear to spike as national elections near, but given the two-year electoral cycle for the U. S. House, and the modern non-stop electioneering process for all candidates regardless of office tenure, there have been few respites in the national debates over public-land management since the 1968 publication of Gates' seminal work.

As a case in point, consider the impact of the 2010 congressional elections, in which the Republican Party re-captured the House of Representatives. No sooner had the ballots been certified than its designees to chair the relevant oversight committees and subcommittees began to ramp up their attacks on the public-land agencies, questioning their management, proposing to slash their budgets, and floating the possibility that the states would prove better stewards of these forests, grasslands, and parks. Annoyed by the Wilderness and Endangered Species acts, incoming chair of the subcommittee on public lands, Rep. Rob Bishop of Utah, starting chipping away at their impact on landscape management by alleging that they undercut national security along the U.S.-Mexico border. "It is unacceptable that our federal lands continue to serve as drug trafficking and human smuggling superhighways," he declared in December 2010, concluding that along the 1,933-mile border "[s]trict environmental regulations are enabling a culture of unprecedented lawlessness."[5]

His colleague, Cynthia Lummis, similarly lambasted the federal government's legal obligations and moral responsibilities for protecting the national forests, parks, and refuges: "Every day our nation's border patrol fights to protect our country against increasingly sophisticated criminal networks that produce and smuggle illegal drugs, and people, into America," she argued in June 2011. "Unfortunately, DOI policies have tied the hands of Border Patrol agents, who need access to federal lands to carry out their constitutional responsibility to secure the border." To unfetter them, Lummis proposed, and the Republican-controlled House passed, an amendment preventing the Department of Homeland Security from transferring funds to the Department of Interior to mitigate any damage resulting from its actions in designated wilderness areas. Although such mitigation is required by federal law, and is standard practice between governments and agencies on the local, state, and national levels, the Republican supporters of this amendment ignored such claims, cheering its anti-environmentalism, its alleged capacity to stop the "further bloating of the federal estate."[6]

Congressional budget-slashers also targeted these various regulatory institutions—the BLM, Forest Service, Park Service, and Fish and Wildlife Service—to cripple their ability to do their job of managing the full array of remarkable resources under their care. As a result, the public lands became a pawn in the quite bruising federal-budget battle in the spring of 2011. So intense was the partisan debate that for a time it appeared as if the federal government would be forced to shut down, locking up the public lands. In the end, that did not happen, and the deal that President Obama brokered with Congress initially seemed to maintain critical environmental protections. The administration's defensive maneuvers even earned it quick praise from mainstream green organizations. Scott Slesinger, legislative director of the Natural Resources Defense Council, made the case: "President Obama, Senate Majority Leader Harry Reid, and many senators deserve the American people's gratitude for standing firm against the nineteen anti-environment riders pushed by the Republican leadership and the Tea Party extremists."

Alas, these lauded politicians had not stood quite as firmly as their green supporters first believed. When the details of these rough budget negotiations finally emerged, for instance, they revealed that the fiscal cuts and policy compromises that Democratic negotiators had accepted established some troubling precedents for the public lands and the species they sheltered.

Start with wolves. Their presence has long rankled western ranchers convinced that these animals' existence is in direct competition with their livestock operations. Since the late nineteenth century, they have wrangled substantial federal support for their convictions. The old U. S. Biological Survey (now Wildlife Services in the Department of Agriculture) offered hired hunters bounties to kill wolves; its actions were later codified in the Animal Damage Control Act (7 U.S.C. §§ 426-426c) that President Herbert Hoover signed in March 1931. These mandates underwrote a brutally successful extirpation campaign. By the 1930s, wolves—and a lot of other critters—had been cleared from valley, basin, and range.

With the enactment of the Endangered Species Preservation Act (1966), later expanded through the Endangered Species Act (1973), Congress began to reverse its previous commitment to these animals' extermination. These new protections required public-land bureaus to maintain habitat for those species that the U. S. Fish and Wildlife Service certified were threatened or endangered. In time, scientists and activists began arguing for the reintroduction of some of those animals, including wolves, bears, and coyotes, that once had been shot, poisoned, and trapped on the public domain.

Initial recovery programs have demonstrated some success, and yet with every sighting of a healthy new wolf pack opposition to their reintroduction has become more vocal and targeted. Since the late 1980s, these opponents have fused their rhetoric with the region's longstanding antipathy to the federal government's legal obligations to protect and manage the public domain. Shooting wolves, really and metaphorically, has been a way to stick it to Uncle Sam.

This hostility found curious presidential sanction during the 2011 budget crisis. President Obama signed off on a controversial provision to turn wolf management over to the respective states that Senator Jon Tester (D-MT) and Rep. Mike Simpson (R-ID) had stuck into the budget agreements. Said Tester: "This wolf fix isn't about one party's agenda. It's about what's right for Montana and the West—which is why I've been working so hard to get this solution passed, and why it has support from all sides. It's high time for a predictable, practical law that finally delists Montana's wolves and returns their management to our state—for the sake of Montana jobs, our wildlife, our livestock, and for the sake of wolves themselves." What Tester did not acknowledge was that the real "fix" that this provision provided was to his sagging election prospects. To shore them up amid a tough political cycle for western Democrats, the Obama administration willingly stripped this endangered animal of its ESA protections at the very moment when its recovery seemed assured. As has been recorded in the long and bloody history of human predation on wolves, this magnificent animal took a very big hit. Concluded Jeff Ruch, executive director of Public Employees for Environmental Responsibility: "This gave Jon Tester a powerful political pelt to hang on his wall."[7]

Tester dismissed those who projected that his maneuver would lead to other attempts to de-list endangered or threatened species. "We didn't amend the Endangered Species Act. We asked that a recovered species-a species that [FWS] projected at 300 when it was reintroduced and now is 1,700, be taken off and managed just how we manage elk and mule deer and antelope and everything else." The ink was barely dry on the provision, however, before Senators John Cornyn (R-TX) and James Inhofe (R-OK) pushed amendments to the Economic Revitalization Act of 2011 to prohibit USFWS from listing the dune sagebrush lizard and the lesser prairie chicken. The Tester-Simpson amendment, then, set a precedent and, in Ruch's perspective, sent "a signal that, as far as the Obama administration is concerned, the Endangered Species Act is a bargaining chip."[8]

The gamble emboldened Republicans in Congress further to challenge the Obama administration's public-lands legislative agenda. One example of many: they prevented the BLM from creating an inventory of lands that had the potential to be designated as protected wilderness. This action was designed to gauge how committed the president was to the preservation of those priceless wild lands that earlier he had identified as key features in his much-ballyhooed program, "America's Great Outdoors." Announced with great fanfare in February 2011, the initiative hoped to reconnect Americans with their rich natural environs: "Despite our conservation efforts," the president asserted, "too many of our fields are becoming fragmented, too many of our rivers and streams are becoming polluted, and we are losing our connection to the parks, wild places, and open spaces we grew up with and cherish." Of equal concern was that "[c]hildren, especially, are spending less time outside running and playing, fishing and hunting, and connecting to the outdoors just down the street or outside of town."[9] These sentiments scanned nicely, but the depth of the chief executive's political commitment to these galvanizing words emerged when, within a month of uttering them, he sacrificed essential portions of his back-to-nature proposal.

This recap of some the arguments that erupted over America's public lands during the first months of the 112th Congress reminds us that these treasured spaces have never been and can never be apolitical. Owned in common, managed via congressionally sanctioned laws that the Supreme Court has fully sustained, the national forests and grasslands, parks and preserves are funded through federal tax receipts; the public lands are thus national in scope and significance. And their controversial histories reinforce as well the idea that they have always been vulnerable to shifting tides of public opinion, alterations in fiscal support, overlapping authorities for their management, involving federal, state, even local, mandates, as well as critical tribal prerogatives and military claims. On the map and through a bureaucratic flow-chart their very presence seems to defy logic and reason. But never doubt their reality in the political arena or in the hearts and minds of those who live in and around them; who recreate along their up-country trails, wetlands, or marshes, in thick forest or open water; who mine or log or harvest some of their natural resources; or who may never visit them but are grateful for their existence, for the possibility of their plenty.

It is with this array of contests, accommodations, and politics that *Public Lands, Public Debates* is primarily concerned. Using the Forest Service as a marker of the broader debates Americans have engaged in since the late nineteenth century, the book examines moments high and low, public and private, that help explain some of the particular (and occasionally peculiar) tensions that have shaped the context in which the agency has operated. Like those, for instance, that led to its birth. The first section of this volume, Creative Forces, teases out some of the intellectual sources, political maneuverings, and cultural resonances that ultimately led to the formation of a federal bureau dedicated to the conservative management of the nation's forests and grasslands. To build a consensus in support of this idea required the publication of a seminal text, George Perkins Marsh's *Man and Nature* (1864), but although the book said a great deal about the need for Americans to steward their natural resources before it was too late, it did not urge the creation of a governmental agency with stewardship as its mission. How Marsh's insight impelled Franklin B. Hough, Nathaniel Egleston, F. P. Baker, and the multi-talented George Bird Grinnell to work front and center and behind the scenes to promote a federal commitment to forestry and conservation is critical in its own right. But this activism, so at odds with Congress' historic attempts to reduce the size of the public domain, sparked a strong pushback from states-rights proponents in and out of Washington, D. C. These early forest reformers were also overtaken within the very movement they launched by such figures as Bernhard

Fernow and more aggressively by Gifford Pinchot, first chief of the U. S. Forest Service. Both men were trained foresters who joined in common cause with those less well credentialed and the voluntary associations such as the American Forest Association that these individuals had founded to advance their claims. But the claims of scientific expertise that these foresters wielded meant that the amateurs' days were numbered. So Pinchot signaled when he and his family underwrote the country's first graduate school in forestry at Yale; established a professional organization, the Society of American Foresters, whose membership depended on holding the requisite academic degree; and then preferentially hired those educated in the new discipline.

This new order was not without its critics. The assertion that the Forest Service would enact a science-based managerial ethos for the national forests (a name they acquired in 1907) provoked a series of Sagebrush Rebellions. Since the early twentieth century, western ranchers, loggers, and livestock operators, and their local, state, and national political representatives, have revolted against the imposition of regulations and user fees associated with their desire to exploit relevant resources on the public lands. In the final decades of the twentieth century these episodic challenges came paired with sharp rebuttals from the political left; environmental activists rebuked the Forest Service and those interest groups they were convinced had captured the agency and co-opted its mission. These oppositional claims, in the context of the Reagan administration's anti-environmentalism, at times turned violent, damaging the civic arena.

Violence was not the only option, of course. At the same time that Congress was debating passage of the Wilderness Act and Aspinall was negotiating with the White House to sanction the Public Land Law Commission's wholesale evaluation of the federal land-management efforts, a private-public partnership emerged. In 1963, Gifford Pinchot's son and family donated the late forester's ancestral home, Grey Towers, to the Forest Service. They did not want it to become a museum reifying his achievements but a center for public engagement on critical issues confronting the public lands, as well as on the health and well-being of the citizenry who depended on these resources. Focused first on conservation education, then on environmental-forestry research, and later still on environmental policy analysis and collaborative conservation, and until the 1990s suffering from uneven funding and commitment, the Pinchot Institute for Conservation nonetheless has held firm to the idea that President John Kennedy gave voice to in September 1963 when he dedicated the institute from the front steps of Grey Towers:

> Conservation is the key to the future, and I believe our future can be bright. If we can continue to expand the programs we have begun—if all of us at every level can meet our responsibilities—if we can gain new insight and foresight from the Pinchot Institute and similar centers of learning—then we can write for our land a record of accomplishment and high purpose unparalleled in the world.[10]

The president was assassinated two months later, but his testimonial, and its representative claim on the wider culture's growing appreciation of the need to address the nation's environmental ills, lives on in the passage of a slew of congressional legislation that occurred shortly after his assassination, from the Wilderness Act (1964) and National Trails System Act (1968) to the National Environmental Policy Act (1970) and the Clean Air and Water acts of the 1970s. The states were busy, too. A record of their commitment is illustrated in the institutionalization of the idea of conservation in agencies and bureaus now dedicated to the management of their public lands and the recreational opportunities and natural resources they contain. Their proliferation and disparate missions test the meaning of the term "conservation" or "environmental," a rhetorical challenge that illuminates how difficult it is to talk about our collective relationship to the public lands, as idea and fact.

It only seems that the past had a better handle on these semantics, that its path was better blazed by word and deed. But it did not, which is a key theme in the section Policy Schemes. Take, for instance, the knock-down, drag-out fights over the passage of the Antiquities Act (1906) and the Weeks Act (1911). It took years for their proponents to define their terms, to build the requisite political coalitions needed to enact these seminal pieces of legislation. Yet even if the Antiquities Act granted presidents unchecked power to create national monuments, that authority did not tamp down controversy about their actions and did not necessarily alter the on-the-ground management of such sites as Devils Tower. As complicated was the reception accorded the Weeks Act, which gave the executive branch the capacity to purchase land to create national forests. It took eleven years for Congress to approve the law, a span of time that was required to resolve what its sharpest critics believed was a constitutional logjam: what right did the federal government have to buy private property from willing sellers?

The question rankled those staunchly opposed to the potential expansion of the federal estate; these were only satisfied after Forest Service lawyers linked land purchases in high-country watersheds to the interstate rivers they fed, and thus connected them to the federal oversight articulated in the Commerce Clause of the Constitution. The Weeks Act, ironically enough, also placed the federal government in the position to buy back land that many decades earlier had resided in the public domain.

That the past is ever present, that its presence can be traced physically in the land itself and in people's shifting decisions about how to manage it, is the subject of chapters assessing what Pinchot dubbed the Bloody Angle, the contentious issue of grazing on the public lands, and the Supreme Court decisions that ultimately granted the Forest Service the power to regulate this use. It is found, too, in the interwoven histories—geological and human—of a place called Devils Postpile National Monument; in the longstanding commitment to fight wildland fires in the treacherous San Gabriel Mountains of Southern California; in the rearguard actions to gain a handle on the expanding and illegal production of marijuana on the national forests, particularly in the Golden State. This reciprocal relationship between time past and time present also appears in the policy dilemmas associated with major changes in forest property ownership in the American west; as more and more timber companies sell off their landed assets, fragmenting ownership patterns, this dramatic turn of events will have critical implications for how (or if) federal agencies will be able to manage the public lands on a landscape-scale level.

These various tensions have sparked as well a series of uncomfortable questions about the Forest Service's continued existence. It is not immediately clear, for example, that the present configuration of this land-management agency offers the best structure for meeting the many challenges of the twenty-first century. Surely the national forests would benefit from a rethinking of the bureaucratic systems that preceding generations devised to govern their use. It is at least well worth exploring the extent to which these historic arrangements should continue to shape contemporary action in an age of dynamic climate change.

Yet any such thinking ahead must include the backward glance, not least because some of the recent inner tensions that have rocked the Forest Service, which are the focus of the book's third section, have hampered its ability to reconceive of its place in the political landscape. I was fortunate to have a good seat from which to watch some of this tumult, for in 2004-

05, as the agency celebrated its one hundredth birthday, I served as its centennial lecturer, crisscrossing the country to deliver more than seventy public lectures on some of the environmental benefits derived from its first century of service and political controversies that had erupted during that period. Visiting every one of the Forest Service's nine regions, speaking before audiences tiny (six people in Cordova, Alaska) and large (nine hundred in Jacksonville, Florida), and in places as distinct and distant as Plymouth, New Hampshire, Asheville, North Carolina, and Riverside California, Cloquet, Minnesota, Monticello, Arkansas and Lufkin, Texas—I met with seasonal workers, rangers, supervisors and regional foresters, industry reps and grassroots activists. And listened.

I had not realized that listening would be the most important element of my year of speaking. But whatever I thought I was doing when I stood up in a university lecture hall, or at a conference podium, a forest visitor center, or local historical society, the audience had other ideas. For them, my talks on the agency's contested past were but prelude to Q&A. That is when they weighed in on the hot-button issues then roiling management of national forests named Chugach, Lolo, or Coconino; Rio Grande, Nantahala, or Wallowa-Whitman. Clearcutting and riparian habitats; grazing and water quality; salmon, salmon, salmon; fire—prescribed, wildland, or arson; all creatures great and small, endangered or threatened; GMO trees, the decline in rural timber-based economics; and lack of toilet paper at trailhead toilets. There was no question that these forests and grasslands were beloved; the passion they evoked made it clear that the surrounding hamlets, suburbs, and cities had laid claim to them; these public lands are decidedly public—ours.

But just who was the preferred "our" was, well, that was a matter of heated debate. Regardless of who opened the discussion—policy wonk or naïf; grizzled timber beast or wide-eyed environmentalist; rafter or dam-builder; rider of horses or ATVs—the oppositional voices went straight to the microphone (or just stood up and started in). The disputes could be well mannered, if ideological. Heart-felt anger could become theatrical. And people laughed: unexpectedly, sarcastically, happily. Yet whatever the tenor of the exchange, it occurred to me I was overhearing a community's intimate conversation with itself, much like one-time telephone switchboard operators must have done as they connected households on a party line.

However routinized some of the back-and-forth came to be, the experience also sensitized me to the sheer range of conundrums that the national forests embodied, and just how numerous were the people who were seeking their resolution. Watching democracy at work can be bewildering, even frustrating, but the only way individuals and organizations can sift through the often messy business of public deliberation is to deliberate. As part of my contribution to this process, I began to write a series of essays that tracked these debates and arguments. About the hope and hesitations that the Healthy Forest Restoration Act (2003) had generated across the national forest system. About why downstream interests must pay close attention to the water flowing off the national forests, especially in the oft-arid west. I suggested that voters might want to be more aware of the political pressures that can buffet the Forest Service, and that they might become a bit more savvy about the intensifying collaboration that was emerging in public-lands management, a trend that ran counter to the conflicts that dominated the public discourse about them. In play at the same time were the Forest Service's musings about its organizational identity related to its status within the Department of Agriculture, reevaluations that led to the revision of some of its operating objectives. Perhaps among the most salient was the recognition that its provision of environmental services—what in 2004 Associate Chief Sally Collins called the national forests' "natural capital"—was a return to its founding principles and a newfound calling.[11]

Collins, who five years later became the first director of what is now the USDA's Office of Environmental and Markets, also pushed the Forest Service to look beyond its territorial domain, beyond our national borders. Although the agency always had paid attention to the global dimensions of forest management, following Gifford Pinchot's internationalist lead, it reemphasized its external perspective in the first years of the twenty-first century. In response to the Seventh American Forest Congress (1998), and the push from that assembly for more community-based forestry, Collins and her colleagues began to trek to Oaxaca, Mexico, to study its integrative models of communal land management. Southern Mexico had a lot to teach northern Montana.[12]

And me: I had participated in the congress and was struck by the glimmering possibilities that the quest for great local management contained. This concept gained academic credence for me a couple of years later as I edited a special issue of *Environmental History* on the history and present state of community-forestry programs in Asia.[13] That abroad I might discover some answers to what seemed like age-old questions plaguing the

U.S. public lands seemed clear in 2002, during a transformative visit to the Tiputini Biodiversity Station in the heart of the Ecuadoran Amazon.

I became more convinced when, at Collins' invitation, I attended the second and third MegaFlorestais conferences as part of the support staff. The ten countries that make up this informal organization are home to two-thirds of the world's forested estate, and the leaders of their public-land agencies use the annual meeting as a chance to talk about the difficulties they are encountering. In 2007, the group meet in St. Petersburg, Russia, a week after the Nobel Peace Prize was bestowed on the Intergovernmental Panel on Climate Change and Vice President Al Gore, and much of the formal presentations and corridor chatter was dominated by the formative role that climate change—its meteorological realities and environmental consequences—would have in shaping the management strategies of China and Russia, Indonesia, Democratic Republic of Congo, and Australia, Canada, and the United States.[14]

That same conversation picked right up, seemingly in mid-sentence, at the 2008 sessions held in the Brazilian cities of Brasilia and Manaus: there the representatives considered the best ways by which better to manage their forest resources, and thus their societies' carbon footprints; land-tenure reforms that allowed greater local control were at the top of the list. Another teachable moment came after a night-long sail down the Amazon from Manaus to the river port of Itacoatiara, where the group reconvened on the property of Precious Woods Amazon, a European funded logging operation. The company's rigorous environmental controls and its deep commitment to community well-being is a sterling example of how to meld conservative forestry, economic development, and social justice, a local example for how to work deliberately, conscientiously, in a globalized marketplace. We have much to learn.

Notes

1. Wayne N. Aspinall, "Foreword," in Paul W. Gates, *History of Public Land Law Development* (Washington, D. C.: Government Printing Office, 1968), iii.
2. James Lawrence Powell, *Dead Pool: Lake Powell, Global Warming, and the Future of Water in the West*, (Berkeley: University of California Press, 2008), p. 115.
3. Gates, *History of Public Land Law Development*, 1-3; Gates writes from an English-only perspective, paying scant attention to the tribes' place in this land-grab process, and almost none to the impact of the French and Spanish colonial land laws and subsequent property-rights issues that as a result have emerged.
4. Ibid, 32.
5. Stephanie Simon, "Wilderness Policy Sparks Western Ire," *Wall Street Journal*, December 30, 2010: http://online.wsj.com/article/SB1000142405274870454300

4576051981953491522.html?mod=googlenews_wsj; last accessed July 21, 2011; Rob Bishop, press release, December 15, 2010: http://robbishop.house.gov/News/DocumentSingle.aspx?DocumentID=217552; last accessed July 21, 2011.

6. Cynthia Lummis, press release, June 2, 2011; http://lummis.house.gov/News/DocumentSingle.aspx?DocumentID=244390; last accessed, July 21, 2011.

7. Charles Taylor, "Budget's Wolf Delisting Opens Pandora's Box of Species Attacks, Enviro Groups Warn," *New York Times*, April 13, 2011; http://www.nytimes.com/gwire/2011/04/13/13greenwire-budgets-wolf-delisting-opens-pandoras-box-of-s-99159.html; last accessed June 16, 2011.

8. Ibid.

9. http://americasgreatoutdoors.gov/2011/02/15/president-obama-launches-initiative-to-develop-a-21st-century-strategy-for-america%E2%80%99s-great-outdoors/; last accessed on June 16, 2011.

10. http://www.foresthistory.org/ASPNET/Places/GreyTowers/JFK_speech.pdf; last accessed July 20, 2011.

11. Sally Collins, "Environmental Services: Making Conservation Work," Outdoor Writers of America, June 22, 2004: http://www.fs.fed.us/news/2004/speeches/06/environmental-services.shtml; last accessed June 21, 2009.

12. "USDA Announces New Office of Ecosystem Services and Markets," December 8, 2008 press release: http://www.usda.gov/wps/portal/usda/usdahome?contentid=2008/12/0307.xml&contentidonly=true; last accessed June 23, 2011; on outcomes of the Seventh American Forest Congress, see: http://www.yale.edu/forest_congress/; last accessed June 23, 2011.

13. Special Issue: "Forest History in Asia," *Environmental History*, April 2001.

14. Char Miller, "'The Wolf is at the Door': Forests, Foresters, and Global Climate Change," *Journal of Forestry*, January/February 2008, 5-6.

CREATIVE FORCES

This section explores the emergence of the idea of conservation in the United States; probes some of the key political, social, and intellectual dilemmas that confronted those who advocated for the protection or preservation of the nation's public lands; and does so by analyzing the contributions of such little-known figures as Nathaniel Egleston and Albert Potter as well as those who need little introduction, such as George Perkins Marsh and Gifford Pinchot. The range of subjects is as diverse, including the late-nineteenth-century debates over the professionalization of knowledge; the creation of what came to be called national forests; the long-running arguments over rangeland management; and the eruption of sagebrush rebellions past and present that called into question the emergence of the modern nation-state as heralded in the 1905 establishment of the Forest Service.

Le Coup D'Oeil Forestier
SHIFTING VIEWS OF FEDERAL FORESTRY IN AMERICA,
1870-1945

Lucien Boppe, assistant director of L'Ecole nationale forestière in Nancy, France, made a "tremendous impression" on Gifford Pinchot. The young American student, the first to attend classes at the venerable French forestry school, was captivated by Boppe, a man of short and stocky stature with immense vitality, a teacher who had "a great contempt for mere professors," for he had "learned in the woods what he taught in the lecture room." His lectures made forestry come to life, Pinchot remembered, made it "visible," a visibility reinforced when he took his students into the woods. "We measured single trees and whole stands, marked trees to be cut in thinnings, and otherwise practiced the duties of a forester." Such work, Pinchot later recalled, "was far more valuable than any reading."[1]

Just as invaluable was another lesson he absorbed from his French mentor: "the master quality of the forester," Boppe assured Pinchot, is "*le coup d'oeil forestier*—the forester's eye, which sees what it looks at in the woods." This form of insight was as environmental in focus as it was political in vision. Trained to acquire an in-depth understanding of the woods, foresters, to practice their craft, must put their knowledge to work, creating wealth from board-feet harvested. That's why Boppe also told Pinchot that when "you get home to America you must manage a forest and make it pay."[2]

Sound advice, no doubt, but advice that presumed a society and politics committed to intensive land management of the kind Boppe taught and on the scale that France (and other European countries) enacted. Such did not pertain in the United States, either prior to Pinchot's departure for France in 1889 or upon his return a year later. So little did his fellow citizens understand of Pinchot's new profession that a well-meaning woman, hearing of his European studies, remarked: "So you are a forester! How very nice! Then you can tell me just what I ought to do about my roses."[3]

Her confusion of forestry with gardening, matched by Pinchot's perplexity as to how to respond, is an important reminder of the complications that can come with the cross-cultural transfer of ideas. Pinchot recognized that the importation of forestry to his native ground would be difficult, and not just because of his encounter with one clueless person. Over the preceding three decades, many other Americans had confronted the same misconceptions or, worse, outright rejection of the kind of state-regulated land management that forestry entailed. He knew too that without this earlier generation of conservation activists, his prospects for establishing governmental forestry were dim. Without them, he would not be able to employ his freshly trained forester's eye.

One of those on whom Pinchot's future depended was German forester Bernhard E. Fernow. He had come to the United States in 1876 to attend the U.S. Centennial Exposition in Philadelphia, as an official Prussian observer to the celebration of American Independence, and most likely to attend the concurrent sessions of the second annual meeting of the American Forestry Association. He stayed, married his American fiancée, whom he had earlier met in Germany, and sought work commensurate with his training. There was little to be found, but by 1886 he had been named the third chief of the U. S. Division of Forestry. Fernow's life story neatly embodied the westward migration of European ideas in the 1870s that would do so much to introduce forestry to the American mind and landscape.[4]

That decade marks the beginning of a remarkable period during which the United States proved particularly receptive to a host of European notions about the proper role of the government in setting national policy. Until the early 1940s, the "reconstruction of American social politics" was intimately bound up with "movements of politics and ideas throughout the North Atlantic world that trade and capitalism had tied together," historian Daniel T. Rodgers has argued. "This was not an abstract realization, slumbering in the recesses of consciousness. Tap into the debates that swirled throughout the United States and industrialized Europe over the problems and miseries of 'great city' life, the insecurities of wage work, the social backwardness of the countryside, or the instabilities of the market itself, and one finds oneself pulled into an intense, transnational traffic in reform ideas, policies, and legislative devices." To make this "Atlantic era in social politics" possible required the creation of a "new set of institutional connections" with European societies, "new brokers" who would facilitate the intellectual exchange, and a cultural shift that would allow Americans to suspend, perhaps for the first (and only) time, its "confidence in the peculiar dispensation of the United States from the fate of other nations."[5]

In his compelling analysis, Rodgers makes only the briefest mention of forestry, and it is a late reference at that: in 1936 "a delegation of public foresters, including the chief of the U.S. Forest Service himself," were among those whose travel to Germany the Oberlaender Trust underwrote, funneling these "social policy experts through the familiar stations of German social progress." They may have been the last of such delegations. Yet over the preceding sixty years, the number of formal and informal exchanges had been continuous and of crucial importance to the development of the American forestry, none more so than the arrival in the United States in 1876 of that first, essential cultural broker, Bernhard Fernow.[6]

He was not the only participant in this rich trans-Atlantic cultural process, and given that Rodgers' model depends on an *American* hunger for European knowledge, perhaps he is not the best marker of it; he brought his technical knowledge of forestry with him. Other Americans of the 1870s who were concerned about the rapid devastation of the nation's wooded estate, and who believed that European scientific forestry might correct this difficult problem, had to seek out the relevant information. They avidly read British and German forestry texts, corresponded with their authors, joined the recently formed (1875) American Forestry Association or similar organizations that gave them access to additional information on European forestry, and traveled abroad to learn directly from European foresters. In so doing, they testified to the power of ideas to change social policy and alter political behavior.

For this cohort, there was much that needed changing. As early beneficiaries of the industrial revolution, they were also acutely aware of its remarkable and unrestrained consumption of wood. To generate the steam necessary to power industrial machinery and the new transportation mechanisms, as well as to construct the massive new cities and shore up innumerable mines, required the clearcutting of once-bountiful forests; wholesale harvesting spread from the Great Lakes to the south and later to the Rocky Mountains and Pacific coast. As the trees crashed down, alarmed voices rose up. The *Sacramento Daily Union* warned in 1878 that if the then-current rate of logging continued unchecked, "the exhaustion of the forest growth in the Sierra is only a question of some ten years, and ... if the rate of consumption is increased the catastrophe will occur considerably sooner." Similarly vexed was Interior Secretary Carl Schurz, who a year earlier had predicted that it was only a matter of time before the nation's dire shortage of wood would jeopardize its capacity to build new homes. A timber famine seemed at hand.[7]

Even as observers fretted over this dangerous possibility, and projected a catastrophe that would rival the fall of the ancient civilizations of the Mediterranean—they easily compared the future of the United States with a treeless (and impotent) Greece—these images of doom led some to ponder how best to change the status quo. One of those was Franklin B. Hough, a physician and statistician, who understood forestry to be "a composite of natural history, geology, mathematics, and physics." From his New York State home, Hough had been assessing census reports that reflected what those involved in the lumber business already knew—that extensive harvests had depleted most eastern and Great Lake forests, and that southern and western woods were now under assault. This economic fact required a social prescription, the good doctor believed, and in 1873 he presented his findings in a paper entitled "On the Duty of Governments in the Preservation of Forests" to the American Association for the Advancement of Science. That governments had such an obligation was a radical departure for a nation wedded to laissez-faire capitalism. But Hough's reading in the scientific literature, his visits to Europe, and his long-standing correspondence with German forester Dietrich Brandis offered him access to different models of governance; these allowed him to suggest alternatives to the rapid transfer of public wooded lands to corporate interests or homesteaders.[8]

The text he most depended on was George Perkins Marsh's seminal volume, *Man and Nature: The Earth as Modified by Human Action* (1864), which the American diplomat had written while living in Italy. Marsh (and, by extension, Hough) was persuaded that deforestation of the European landscape had been responsible for the decline and fall of its great civilizations; he was equally persuaded that the only way to reverse this process—which he and Hough feared the United States was in danger of replicating—was to understand the close link between human profligacy and woodland devastation. To restrain human consumption of natural resources, to abate "the restless love of change which characterizes us," Marsh proposed the adoption of a conservative land-management policy to be administered through a paternal form of government reminiscent of France and Germany, the leaders in European forestry.[9]

The wide gap between European energy and American lethargy impelled progressives to petition Congress and succeeding presidents to pass social legislation to protect the citizenry and enhance the commonwealth. For some reformers, Rodgers notes, this led to calls for top-down initiatives focused on better housing, sewage treatment, or efficient transportation. Forest advocates sought legislation to reflect their faith in the duty and capacity of government to regulate resource exploitation. Hough was an assiduous lobbyist and prolific publicist, and his campaigning bore fruit in 1876 when he was appointed to report on the nation's "forest supplies and conditions." The fact of his 650-page document is as critical as the conclusions he reached within it; never before had the federal government published such an in-depth finding on the subject. What Hough found was troubling, but then he expected to be disturbed by the lumber industry's terrible and swift cutting of timber and the resultant scarred and battered terrain; his prior studies had paved the way for this negative reaction.[10]

Another who partly shared Hough's worries was Charles Sprague Sargent, head of the Arnold Arboretum and future publisher of *Garden & Forest*, which would become the central forum in the 1880s for sustained discussions in the U.S. about forestry and conservation. Encouraged by Interior Secretary Carl Schurz, who wanted a detailed analysis for the 1880 Census on the nation's available timber supplies, the Smithsonian Institution hired Sargent to write what would become the *Report on the Forests of North America*; it finally appeared in 1884. Based on Sargent's on-site investigations, it delineated the distribution of tree species and forest densities, and assessed the economic value of the nation's varied woods. Sargent concurred with Hough's assessment that there had been rapid harvesting of timber in New England, the Mid-Atlantic, and Midwestern states, but this evidence was counterbalanced by the fact that the vast forests of the South and Pacific Northwest had yet to be exploited; a timber panic was not yet in the offing.[11]

Yet Sargent's evidence, when read against the historic record of forest devastation in other sections of the United States, suggested the grim outlines of the future, which is why worries about the extent of clearcutting found their parallel in uncertainties about how to restore cut-over land. Lacking the kind of legal authority that enabled European governments to control private landowners, required by federal law to give away the public domain, and therefore sell significant amounts of valuable forested public lands on which it could wield power, and devoid of technical experts, the prospects for forestry in the United States looked bleak. Even though Congress had established a Division of Forestry in the Department of Agriculture in 1881, with Hough as its first head, the small agency had no woods under its control—and would secure none until 1905. The new division's energies were also deflected by internecine struggles that embroiled Hough, his subordinates, and superiors, and that led, in the summer of 1882, to Hough's demotion to the status of an "agent" of the Department of Agriculture. "Feel very low spirited," he scribbled in his diary, "and all my ambition is gone." His depression deepened when, that October, he and a colleague launched the *American Journal of Forestry*, only to suspend its publication eleven months later. Doubtful that anyone read the voluminous reports he had written while in office, convinced that no real change had occurred in the nation's consciousness about the dangers timber devastation posed, he was left to compare unfavorably the differences between European forestry and American lumbering. Those differences once had inspired him and other reformers to enter into the political arena; now they were a painful reminder of how much remained to be done.[17]

His replacement, Nathaniel Egleston, would come to feel similarly. History has not been kind to the second chief of the Division of Forestry in the U. S. Department of Agriculture in good part because his contemporaries were convinced that his hiring was a reflection of Gilded Age corruption. Egleston was appointed to his post in 1883, after Agricultural Commissioner George P. Loring demoted Hough, even though he had amassed nothing like his predecessor's resume. Indeed, the Yale-trained minister had not been schooled in the virtue of trees until after the Civil War. Living among the Taconic Mountains in far northwest Massachusetts, Egleston did not fail to observe that Williamstown, and farming communities like it, battered as they were by wartime loss of life, were shrinking further as young men and women slipped away from the New England countryside for industrial cities, near and far: Springfield, Hartford, and New Haven, like Boston, Providence, and New York, were magnets for youth fleeing crimped, small-town life in search of better work, wider prospects, and brighter lights. As with others of his era, Egleston worried about the Industrial Revolution's influence on landscape and demography; with them he too came to believe that arborculture—tree planting—might help stem the migratory tide.

More beautiful townscapes, he reasoned, would enable the young better to resist the siren call of modernity, a conviction he sketched out in his first major work on what would become an all-consuming subject: *The Home and its Surroundings, or, Villages and Village Life, with Hints for Their Improvement* (1878). For Egleston, there was no tree that more fully dominated the horizon or that could anchor those who might drift away than the stately elm: "Yonder lofty and majestic elm … standing by the side of some farmhouse, which, though ample in size, it dwarfs to a cottage as it rises above it with its dome of shade, and tosses its giant arms high over roof-tree and chimney top! What an object to fill one at the same time with wonder and admiration!" Such billowing rhetoric was not unusual, as Thomas J. Campanella has demonstrated; innumerable late-nineteenth-century provincial hill towns and valley communities—as well as urban behemoths—launched a planting frenzy, which, at its peak, topped twenty-five million elm seedlings. From Williamstown to New Haven (which claimed the title "Elm City"), Sacramento to Buffalo to Keene, New Hampshire (another "Elm City" claimant), *Ulmus americana* had become America's tree. Yet for all its national appeal, its distinctive wine-glass shape was especially associated with New England, becoming, in Campanella's words, "an essential feature in the commodified image of a rural Yankee town."[13]

It was a commodity, Egleston felt certain, that could be and should be transplanted across the American West, regardless of climate, rainfall, or soil. In *Handbook of Tree-planting* (1884), he asserted that "tree planting is almost the first necessity of life" on the Great Plains; without an arboreal domestication of its vastness, "barbarism" would bloom in Kansas and the Dakotas: "Tree planting is almost a first necessity there. The man who settles there should understand that he is to be engaged in a battle with the icy bayonetry of the North, and he needs at once to raise his breastwork of trees to fight behind their cover." Egleston was not alone in preaching arborculture's social virtues and civilizing consequences, but his paeans to a well-wooded country life, and the palpable need to reinvigorate it, when combined with his staunch advocacy of Arbor Day—he was in close contact with J. Sterling Morton who did so much to advance the national celebration of a day of trees—gave him an ever-larger audience in the late 1870s and early 1880s.[14]

"What We Owe to the Trees" (1882) was one of a series of essays he published in major periodicals and in pamphlet form. Each reflects the heavy influence of George Perkins Marsh on Egleston's new-found faith in the necessity for and capacity of human stewardship to restore cut-over and abused lands. "In our own country we have gone to the forest in a kind of freebooter style, cutting and burning more than we could cut, acting for the most part as though all the while in a frolic or a fight, until now at length, after a century or two of this sort of work, we are waking up to the facts that our once boundless woods are disappearing, and that we are likely to suffer no little less thereby," Egleston asserted in his 1882 tract. It "is only the few who seem now to have any adequate sense of our condition as affected by the threatened loss of trees," in whose number he counted himself. To expand the movement required recognition on his readers' part of their role in this destructive impulse and their willingness to convert their silence and complicity into engaged and active protest. If "we are ready to take lessons from the nations that have gone before us," he enthused, "we may escape most of the bitter sufferings which have been their lot. We can do that which will put a period to the evil results of our own misconduct." Although spoken in his words, Egleston actually was giving voice to the insights of George Perkins Marsh; throughout the 1880s the former minister's most seminal role was as a popularizer of Marsh's compelling ethic.[15]

Such work made Egleston popular, too, so much so that he represented Massachusetts at the 1882 American Forest Congress, where he was tapped to be one of the vice presidents of the American Forestry Association. The next year, Agriculture Commissioner Loring elevated Egleston to head the national government's forestry division, giving the sixty-one-year-old retired minister a new, if secular, pulpit.

His tenure was shaky from the start, not least due to the manner of his ascension. Loring's dislike of the previous chief, Franklin Hough, had led him to push Egleston into the top position, and charges swirled that the good reverend had benefited from a bit of backroom politics. These contemporary allegations entered the historical record when a future chief forester, Gifford Pinchot, wrote witheringly in *Breaking New Ground* (1947) that Egleston was "one of those failures in life whom the spoils system is constantly catapulting into responsible positions." Pinchot's retrospective slam was unfair: Egleston had had a distinguished career in the clergy; and he had had precisely as much scientific training in forestry as had Hough—none. But he was so unfavorably compared to Hough because of his lax administrative efforts and vacillating personality.[16]

Consider what transpired after the 1884 presidential election. Grover Cleveland's defeat of Republican James G. Blaine triggered a chain of events within the Department of Agriculture that cast Egleston's failings in sharp relief. Commissioner Loring, a Republican appointee, was replaced by Norman J. Colman, who froze out the forestry chief. Fretting because he could not secure an appointment to meet with his new supervisor, Egleston felt so intimidated that he could not even formulate an agenda for his tiny division, so unclear was he about his status in the new administration. It would have helped had he but asked the commissioner about his future, but he feared to do so; and when Colman finally requested his resignation, and he complied, Colman shocked him by not accepting that which he had just demanded! The new commissioner no doubt figured that he could easily control the manipulable Egleston, a strategy he tested when, without consultation, he hired two additional agents for the Division of Forestry; Egleston failed to protest. His inaction was part of crippling pattern, historian Harold K. Steen has concluded: "Befuddled by indecision and uncertainty, Egleston meekly waited to be fired. He lingered in anguished limbo for three years until relieved by a professional forester, Bernard E. Fernow, in 1886."[17]

That humiliation not withstanding, Egleston remained in the division until Fernow himself retired in 1898. That he preferred to be a subordinate to a supervisor who paid him scant attention, that he reconciled himself to being marginalized in an office over which he once had had jurisdiction, speaks to Egleston's troubled psychological state.

It also illustrates the larger transition then underway in the American forestry movement. In the mid-nineteenth century, all forestry reformers had been self-taught, even the transcendent George Perkins Marsh, whose *Man and Nature* (1864) would define the conservationist ethos for subsequent generations; by the late nineteenth century the world was beginning to belong to the credentialed. Yet these men had pioneered a new profession, created its first national voluntary associations, including the American Forestry Association (AFA) and the American Forest Council, which would subsequently merge with the AFA. They published the initial accountings of the status of the American forests, tried to raise the nation's consciousness about the evils of uncontrolled lumbering, and had even gained some governmental recognition of their concerns through the creation of the forestry division. Without these contributions—however tentative and incomplete—the labor of those who followed would have been that much more difficult.[18]

Among those indebted to this path-breaking work was F. P. Baker, who, two years after Fernow traveled to the United States, had set sail for Europe as one of the U.S. Commissioners to the 1878 Paris Universal Exposition. In the opening to his report on the exhibition of European forestry, he doffed his cap to those on whose scholarship his scant knowledge of the subject depended; he readily acknowledged that his account was "hampered by the reflection that already the whole subject has been ably treated by writers who have brought to bear upon it the resources of immense observation and profound scholarship." Mindful of the attainments of Marsh and Hough, Baker preemptively limited the significance of his observations to an updating of "the history of forestry in Europe to a later period" and the addressing of "hitherto unreported progress." More important, he believed, would be the opportunity once more to "impress upon the American people of the United States the vital importance of the subject of forestry." If they were at all engaged by his account, he would "have accomplished all that can be reasonably expected of him."[19]

The 1878 Paris fair was itself impressive: like other international expositions of the late nineteenth century, it offered participating nations the opportunity to flash their commercial wares, tout their industrial might, and demonstrate how they exemplified the virtues of rationality, progress, and civilization, values which, as the event's title asserted, were presumed "universal." Emblematic of these cultural displays was the magnificent French pavilion on forestry, known as "The Chalet." Built "entirely of woods grown in France, at least two hundred varieties being used in its construction," the striking edifice housed geological and entomological collections maintained at the French national school of forestry, as well as "maps, plans, photographs, and models representing the processes of reforesting mountains and of retaining the shifting surface of sand hills." Most stunning was a Disney-like model of mountain forestry that was set within The Chalet: trudging up a "zigzag track" carved into a fabricated hillside were workers "dressed in the peculiar costume of the country"; on their backs were heavy sleds. When they reached the peak, they loaded logs on the sleds, and sent them down a "timber slide," which curved past charming representations of "the natural features of mountain scenery, the yawning ravines and plunging water-courses." A stunning reflection of the French attention to detail, this display, and others that graphically demonstrated their investment in reforestation and afforestation, convinced Baker of the great benefits to be derived from "French skill and industry," through which "every foot of earth" was carefully "preserved and patiently and laboriously cultivated." Improvident Americans had much to learn from their thrifty European compatriots.[20]

Whether Americans could replicate the successes of French conservation was another matter, for governing land management in France was a strict set of laws that granted governmental jurisdiction over the forests of the public domain, as well as communal woods and private woodlots; its administrative structures, rigorous training for foresters in the national forest schools, and stiff penalties associated with timber poaching or careless handling of the forest, amazed the American commissioner. The existence of a rational landscape and disciplined people, Baker quoted a French writer approvingly, enabled the "forest corps" to take "its place beside the great public services" whose futures would be determined "by the scientific skill and industry which characterizes our age."[21]

But neither law nor custom controlled industrialization's excesses in the United States, a point of some disappointment to Baker. Although he did not propose that his native land adopt uncritically European legal models and technical training, he was clearly fascinated by how the French and Germans, British, Scandinavians, and Swiss were able to regulate the exploitation of natural resources so as to build up their national treasuries even while protecting the land. By contrast, Americans were "famous destroyers of the forest," devastating "thousands of acres of noble forest trees ... merely to rid the earth of them. The Western pioneer," Commissioner Baker concluded, "has passed his life in toilsome labor of chopping and burning trees which his descendants would gladly replace."[22]

Absent a strong central state, and without cultural support for conservation, what "can we do to preserve and restore our forests, to repair the waste of the past, and provide for the needs of the future?" Baker's answer was couched in language that revealed the limitations he believed would prevent European forestry—for all its strengths and prospects—from being easily transplanted to American soil. Although he acknowledged that in the United States of late "a growing sentiment has sprung up in favor of the preservation and cultivation of trees both for ornament and use," he was not yet convinced the public would support the level of governmental "interference" that gave European foresters such unrestrained authority. He doubted, moreover, that legislative mandates were "efficacious" in any event: "few statutes have been more persistently violated," Baker observed dryly, than the already extant ones prohibiting "cutting timber on government land."[23]

It is odd therefore that he put his faith in the U.S. Timber Culture Act of 1873, one of the most persistently violated of federal laws. Designed to encourage prairie homesteaders to plant trees on 40 acres of a 160-acre tract to meet residency requirements and facilitate subsequent ownership, the law had no appreciable effect except, that is, in wooded areas, where the act became a vehicle for fraudulent claims that enabled corporations to clearcut timber without charge. Still, Baker was convinced that what salvaged this act was its political acceptability: it did not promote forestry through "repressive" means, but by holding out "substantial inducements for the cultivation of trees, [it] becomes the patron and encourager of forestry, and thus fosters a popular sentiment in favor of tree-growing. Democracy could be pushed only so far."[24]

For Baker, push came to shove in 1884. That year he gave a speech to the American Forestry Congress in which he advocated the withdrawal from sale or entry of federally owned forests draped on either side of the Rocky Mountains so as to protect the headwaters of the Platte, Rio Grande, and Arkansas rivers. Drawing on his earlier observations of European forestry, he now proposed a multifaceted plan to preserve and manage this vast landscape, including the development of schools of forestry and regional forestry experiment stations, and the funding of federal surveys to establish the inventory and value of these timbered lands. He also called for protection against fire and illegal cutting, and the end to low-cost sales of wood harvested on public lands. "Government timber," he advised, "should nowhere be sold at $1.25 an acre. If sold at all a price should be fixed upon it somewhere near its value." Like Hough before him, Baker had reached a point where it was no longer acceptable simply to work within current political constraints. Due to the relentless destruction of the nation's woods, the time had come to mount a more sustained challenge to the status quo.[25]

That challenge would be taken up, and with considerable success, by a new cohort, many of whom were professional foresters who either had emigrated from Europe (Bernhard Fernow and Carl Schenck) or had been trained there (Gifford Pinchot and Henry S. Graves). These men may not have agreed on all points about the course of an American forestry, but as educators, reformers, and activists they taught a wider public about the value of forestry to the commonweal. In their capacity as civil servants, Fernow, and later Pinchot and Graves, also built the bureaucratic apparatus and secured the requisite political authority to establish a national forest policy. This crucial organizational work was reinforced through their contributions to myriad professional organizations; it is significant that one of these, the Society of American Foresters (1900), supplanted the older American Forest Association as the leading voice on forestry affairs.

That said, their achievements were predicated on the previous generation's intellectual commitments and political activism. It was Marsh, Hough, Baker, even Egleston who first engaged in the fertile trans-Atlantic exchange of ideas, who sought out and popularized European forestry; it was they who discovered just how complicated it would be to introduce its principles to an industrializing America. In sparking a civic debate over the future of the nation's forests, they proved instrumental to the coming struggle to restructure the nation's government so as develop new controls over public lands. These early "lovers of the forest," Pinchot later confirmed, "deserve far more credit than they ever got for their public-spirited efforts to save a great natural resource."[26]

He meant what he said, too, but it is also true that Pinchot worked assiduously to contrast professional foresters with earlier grassroots organizers, academics, and intellectuals. As he and his peers laid down the political foundation for the emerging national forest system and the forest service designed to manage these public lands and built up the educational infrastructure to educate the first generation of home-grown scientific foresters, he was at pains to distinguish these mammoth organizational efforts from his predecessors' ultimately fruitless activism. Despite the many meetings they had attended, the articles they had written, and the legislation they had promulgated, despite their impulse to "urge, beg and implore; to preach at, call upon, and beseech the American people to stop forest destruction and practice Forestry," they failed in an all-important and pragmatic respect: "in the year 1891," Pinchot allowed, "there was not ... a single acre of forest under Forestry anywhere in the United States."[27]

Fourteen years later, as Pinchot left government service, there were more than 150 million acres under management of the U. S. Forest Service, which employed hundreds of fire lookouts, forest rangers, and clerical staff, silviculturalists, hydrologists, and range specialists. Pinchot knew well what he and his conservationist colleagues had achieved, and was convinced that their achievement had come as a result of a deliberate decision to choose different tactics, new means to an old end. "Under the circumstances," he recalled, "I had to play a lone hand. I could not join the denudatics," his name for preservationists such as his friend and ally John Muir, "because they were marching up a blind alley." Neither would he cooperate with lumbermen, "because forest destruction was their daily bread. There was nothing left for me but to blaze my own trail." By which he meant to put forestry "into actual practice in the woods, prove that it could be done by proving it, prove that it was practical by making it work." Experimentation, the young forester believed, would demonstrate the virtue of his work and generate essential public support and political sanction.[28]

At the time, he was less confident about his chances for success, and with good reason. He was not as thoroughly educated in forestry as he might have been: "I intended to be a practicing forester all my life, yet I thought I could spare but thirteen months to get ready for my lifework," he wrote more than a half century after he had brought a hasty end to his studies at L'Ecole nationale forestière. He had attended the school at the suggestion of famed German forester Dietrich Brandis, who became an important mentor for Pinchot, as did the school's silviculturalist, Lucien Boppe. And each man cautioned the young American that his desire to return to the United States to put his ideas into practice was premature; he was not well-enough educated, they warned.

He ignored their warning, but its wisdom dawned on him when, after his return to the United States, he was hired as forester for George W. Vanderbilt's vast estate in western North Carolina. Confused as to how to implement forestry management in a landscape with which he had had no experience, he wrote lengthy appeals to his European advisors seeking guidance; in one such epistle to Brandis, he confessed that "the time has come, as you foretold it would, when I begin to feel the scantiness of my preparation."[29]

Pinchot's forestry work also went slowly due to the conditions of the Vanderbilt forests, which suffered from fire and overgrazing, and these factors undercut his reclamation efforts. Moreover, the operation's labor force was untrained and its start-up costs were high, further frustrating Pinchot's initiatives; although he would claim publicly that he had made forestry pay at Biltmore, in fact he operated at a loss.[30]

These manifold problems would lead him privately to acknowledge having "done little in the work of my profession" during his first year there, and he was relieved to move on to New York to begin a career as a consulting forester; thereafter he monitored Biltmore's new forester, the much more thoroughly trained Carl Schenck. This shift in personnel relieved his European mentors, too: "the best thing that Pinchot has done," Brandis confided to forester William Schlich, "is that he secured Schenck for America." Pinchot's self-promotional conception of Biltmore as the cradle of American forestry was a piece of false labor.[31]

Pinchot would give birth to the real thing in succeeding years, but the reality he brought to life was not so much in the development of forestry in the woods as the establishment of its professional standing in society, a critical contribution to its future in a modernizing America. His timing was perfect, for it was in the late nineteenth century that other professions began to determine the requisite education and training, grant the appropriate degrees, and shape the behavior required of their future practitioners. The American Bar Association (1877), like the American Chemical Society (1875), American Historical Association (1884), American Economic Association (1888), and American Sociological Association (1905), established who could claim to be a lawyer or chemist, historian, economist, or sociologist—and, just as important, who could not. Pinchot would seek the same ends for the forestry profession while serving as head of the USDA Division, later Bureau, of Forestry (1898-1905) and then as chief of the Forest Service (1905-1910). Between 1900 and 1905, he was a driving force behind the creation of the three major institutions without which no profession can exist—a professional society, graduate education, and a source of future work.

In 1900, at his grand home located at 615 Rhode Island Avenue in Washington, D.C., Pinchot called to order the first meeting of the Society of American Foresters, an organization that over time would bestow scientific legitimacy on, and structure the ongoing education within, the profession. Pinchot also had a hand in founding the *Journal of Forestry*, which would become the profession's lead journal; it organized and gave value to the scientific research that appeared in its pages, and the practical experience it disseminated every month.

A professional society requires members, naturally enough, and here again Pinchot was instrumental through his family's endowment of the Yale School of Forestry in 1900, establishing the nation's first graduate program. Together with the school's first dean, Henry S. Graves, whom Pinchot had tapped for the job, he contributed to the development of an appropriate curriculum in forestry education and occasionally taught within it. Because all professions must provide hands-on experience for their neophytes, Yale students spent their summers in Milford, Pennsylvania, training outdoors on Pinchot family woodlands, and indoors in classrooms the family constructed in the town. Having completed their training and received their degrees, young foresters would need gainful employment, and the bulk of them would be hired by the federal agency for which Pinchot was the founding chief, the Forest Service.

The agency in turn functioned as an extension of the New Haven campus. An "enthusiastic Yale man," Pinchot sought there to recreate the fraternal life he had cherished while an undergraduate. When he became the head of the Division of Forestry, for instance, he tapped a number of close friends to work with him. Henry Graves (Yale '92) was Pinchot's right-hand man; George Woodward and Phillip Patterson Wells, who graduated with Pinchot in 1889, provided valuable legal services, while fellow classmate Herbert A. Smith lent his editorial skills to the agency's publications; Thomas Sherrard (Yale '97) contributed his considerable forestry acumen to the agency's daily work.[32]

Yalies were also well represented within the rank and file. In 1905, for example, nearly half of those passing the civil service exam in forestry were Yale graduates, a fact that Pinchot reported enthusiastically to his mother. Little wonder then that the USFS was known affectionately as the Yale Club, a club of much collegiate camaraderie that bound together this first generation of American foresters.[33]

Given the significance of Pinchot's organizational activities, and the speed with which they unfolded—from 1898 to 1910—and given the *esprit de corps* and profound sense of mission that Pinchot imparted to the Forest Service, it is hardly surprising that he believed he *was* the profession, and the profession was him.[34]

However understandable, Pinchot's intense psychological identification with forestry would pose problems for his successors. It did not help, either, that his departure from the Forest Service was the result of an explosive confrontation between him and the president of the United States, William Howard Taft. They clashed shortly after Taft had replaced Theodore Roosevelt in 1908, because, in Pinchot's mind, the new president did not share Roosevelt's passion for using the executive branch's clout on behalf of conservationism. News of suspicious coal-field leases in Alaska led Pinchot publicly to confront the administration, forcing his dismissal. In this, Pinchot had practiced as he had preached: the last advisory in the chief forester's "Rules for Public Service" is: "Don't make enemies unnecessarily and for trivial reasons; if you are any good you will make plenty of them on straight honesty and public policy."[35]

Pinchot's shrewd insight and brave words nonetheless left his successors in a bind. Henry Graves, whose European forestry education Pinchot had underwritten, and who had served as his associate forester before becoming dean at the Pinchot-funded Yale School of Forestry, became the second chief. Less provocative and charismatic, Graves understood that the agency's continued existence depended on his ability to rebuild internal morale, re-knit frayed relations with the White House and Congress, and reclaim public confidence, all the while placating an occasionally nettlesome Pinchot. None of this work came easily, and yet despite being hindered by sharp budget cuts and congressional hostility, Graves managed to stabilize the agency, smoothing the way for William B. Greeley to become its third chief in 1920.

Unlike Graves, Greeley immediately picked a series of fights with Pinchot, challenging his still-profound influence on Forest Service; only in this way, Greeley believed, could he reform the organization in his own image. More conservative than the founder, and more comfortable with the corporate Republicanism dominating that era's political arena, Greeley promoted cooperative relationships with the timber and grazing industries; he countered Pinchot's faith in rigorous regulation by advocating through the Clarke-McNary Act (1924) an accommodation with powerful interest groups. When Pinchot rebutted that federal regulatory controls ought to be extended to industrial forestry operations, Greeley blasted his idea as "unAmerican." Years earlier, Greeley had been thrilled to have "lost caste in the temple of conservation on Rhode Island Avenue," a sneering reference to Pinchot's Washington, D. C., manse, and while chief he did little to repair their relationship. His perspectives on the agency's political purpose, social significance, and economic agenda so dominated professional forestry in the 1920s that an embittered Pinchot resigned from the American Forest Association and stopped attending SAF meetings.[36]

Greeley was much less deft in his response to a more serious bureaucratic threat posed by an aggressive National Parks Service (NPS). Founded in 1916, and headed by former advertising executive Stephen Mather, the Parks Service quickly came into its own at the expense of the Forest Service. Proclaiming its mission was to serve the recreational needs of car-crazy American culture, NPS moved rapidly to publicize the national parks and develop highway connections between them. As is it built public (and congressional) support for its services, it used this good will to press its case for managing the national monuments and majestic parklands then under Forest Service control. So effective were Mather and his managers, and so flat-footed did their Forest Service peers appear, that they plucked one gem after another out of the national forest inventory, most notably the spectacular Grand Canyon.

In tapping "the pulse of the Jazz Age," historian Hal Rothman has observed, NPS sold "Americans leisure and grandeur at a time when ... outdoor recreation increased," an understanding of contemporary needs the Forest Service failed to appreciate. While individual employees, such as Arthur Carhart, Aldo Leopold, and Bob Marshall pushed the Forest Service to delineate wilderness areas and promote back-country recreation, in general the agency's goals in the newly competitive environment seemed "undefined and utterly up in the air." Once proactive, the Forest Service had become reactive, a sign of lost momentum.[37]

The Great Depression, ironically enough, offered the agency an opportunity to make up lost ground. Greeley had resigned in 1928, becoming secretary of the West Coast Lumberman's Association—proof of his real allegiances, Pinchot averred; his replacement, Robert Y. Stuart, a Pinchot ally, was chief until 1933, dying in a tragic fall from his Washington office window. Ferdinand Silcox, an adept administrator, then navigated the agency through the hard and harrowing times. Taking full advantage of the large influx of federal dollars flowing through the Civilian Conservation Corps (CCC), among other New Deal-funding mechanisms, the Silcox-led organization purchased millions of acres of abandoned and devastated lands in the south, midwest, and Great Plains. These new forests and grasslands became employment opportunities for CCC enrollees, who planted seedlings, built shelter belts, repaired eroded terrain, and constructed cabins and trails. The can-do agency was in its element, serving as the vigilant custodian of the nation's public lands.

Only to be thrown a curve-ball. In the early 1930s, Interior Secretary Harold Ickes lobbied President Franklin Roosevelt to support the creation of a new cabinet-level Department of Conservation that would absorb all federal land-management agencies, with the Forest Service as its core organization. Convinced that efficiencies would result, the president approved the plan, muzzled the Secretary of Agriculture, Henry Wallace, and had him prevent the Forest Service from defending itself. In need of outside aid and indefatigable allies, Silcox, through Associate Chief Earl Clapp, contacted Gifford Pinchot, then seventy, to crusade on the agency's behalf. He did so gladly, and between 1935 and 1940, Pinchot and Ickes engaged in one of the most bruising bureaucratic brawls in modern U. S. political history. Over the radio, in newspapers and magazines, and from one podium to another, they pounded each other while rallying their supporters. In the end, Pinchot triumphed, a remarkable testament to his in-fighting skills and dogged perseverance.[38]

His victory was not unalloyed. There was a personal cost for at least one high-ranking forester who had cooperated with the old chief's campaign. The president never promoted Earl Clapp beyond "acting chief," a position he had assumed following Silcox's death in 1939, because he was correctly convinced that Clapp had orchestrated the stout resistance to Ickes' transfer scheme. In sacrificing his career for what he conceived to be the greater good, Clapp paid a heavy professional price.

The same could be said about the Forest Service itself. In its fierce fight for survival, it may have missed an important opportunity to engage in serious reconsideration of how conservationism had evolved and how it would implemented in the coming years; it also failed to reflect on the governmental structure best suited to conserve the lands it managed. As it entered the war years, the agency was intact and independent, but it was also insular in orientation. Its insularity would have dire consequences in the aftermath of World War Two, complicating the Forest Service's implementation of new forest-management techniques, damaging its once-vaunted reputation, and hindering its ability to react to massive social changes, especially the emergence of a potent environmental movement. By the 1970s, the Forest Service and the public it served no longer always saw eye to eye.[39]

Notes

1. Gifford Pinchot, *Breaking New Ground*, fourth edition (Washington, D.C.: Island Press, 1998), p. 11.
2. *Ibid.*
3. *Ibid.*, p. 28.
4. Andrew D. Rodgers, *Bernhard Eduard Fernow: A Story of North American Forestry*. Reprint. (Durham: Forest History Society, 1991), p. 17.
5. Daniel T. Rodgers, *Atlantic Crossings: Social Politics in a Progressive Age* (Cambridge: The Belknap Press of Harvard University Press, 1998), p. 3-4.
6. *Ibid.*, p. 421.
7. Donald J. Pisani, "Forests and conservation, 1865-1890," in Char Miller, ed., *American Forests: Nature, Culture, and Politics* (Lawrence: University Press of Kansas), p. 18.
8. Harold K. Steen, *The U.S. Forest Service: A History* centennial edition (Durham: Forest History Society and University of Washington Press, 2004, p. 9.
9. George Perkins Marsh, *Man and Nature: The Earth as Modified by Human Action* (New York: Charles Scribner, 1864), p. 27-80.
10. Steen, *The U.S. Forest Service*, p. 13; see also,Harold Clepper, *Origins of American Conservation* (New York: John Wiley & Sons, 1966).
11. Michael Williams, *Americans and Their Forests: a Historical Geography* (Cambridge: Cambridge University Press, 1989), p. 376-77; C. S. Sargent, *Report on the Forests of North America (Exclusive of Mexico), Vol. 9 of the Tenth Census of the United States* (Washington, D.C.: Government Printing Office, 1884).
12. Franklin B. Hough, *Report upon Forestry*. Washington, D.C.: Government Printing Office, 1878), p. 6-9; Steen, *The U.S. Forest Service*, p. 17.

13. Nathaniel H. Egleston, *The Home and Its Surroundings or Villages and Village Life; with Hints for Their Improvement* (New York: Harper and Brothers, 1884), p. 73; Thomas J. Campenella, *Republic of Shade: New England and the American Elm* (New Haven: Yale University Press, 2003), p. 92-98.

14. Nathaniel H. Egleston, *Handbook of Tree-planting, or, Why to Plant, Where to Plant, What to Plant, How to Plant* (New York: D. Appleton, 1884), p. 22.

15. Ibid., p. 1-26; Blake Gumprecht, "Transforming the Prairie: Early Tree Planting in an Oklahoma Town," *Historical Geography*, 29: 2001, p. 116-34; Nathaniel H. Egleston, "What We Owe to the Trees," *Harper's New Monthly Magazine*, p. 675-87; Nathaniel H. Egleston, *Arbor Day: hits History and Observance* (Washington, D.C.: Government Printing Office, 1896).

16. Andrew Denny Rodgers, III, *Bernhard Eduard Fernow: A Story of North American Forestry*, second edition (Durham: Forest History Society, 1991), p. 86 relates Hough's perfunctory dismissal: "In May 1883 ... I was sent home," he confided to a friend, and kept "doing what I was told ... realizing the utter impossibility of *doing anything to please the Commissioner* [Loring]—or preparing anything that he would accept." Hough died two years later.

17. Harold K. Steen, *The U. S. Forest Service*, p. 20-21.

18. David Lowenthal, *George Perkins Marsh: Prophet of Conservation* (Seattle: University of Washington Press, 2000), p. 428-29; Steen, *The U. S. Forest Service*, p. 9-14.

19. F. P. Baker, *Forestry.* In *Reports of the United States Commissioners to the Paris Universal Exposition, 1878* (Washington, D.C.: Government Printing Office, 1878), vol. 3, p. 391.

20. Rodgers, *Atlantic Crossings*, p. 8-9; Baker, *Forestry*, p. 393-94.

21. Baker, *Forestry*, p. 398.

22. *Ibid.*, p. 423.

23. *Ibid.*

24. Steen, *The U.S. Forest Service*, p. 123; Rodgers, *Fernow*, p.12; Baker, *Forestry*, p. 423.

25. Rodgers, *Fernow*, p. 93.

26. Pinchot, *Breaking New Ground*, p. 29.

27. *Ibid.*

28. *Ibid.*, p. 29-31.

29. *Ibid.*, p. 16-22; Gifford Pinchot to Dietrich Brandis, August 21, 1893, Pinchot Papers, Library of Congress.

30. Gifford Pinchot, *Biltmore Forest* (Chicago: R.R. Donnelly & Sons, 1893).

31. Gifford Pinchot to Mr. Wetmore, March 21, 1893, Pinchot Papers, Library of Congress; William Schlich to Carl Schenck, January 13, 1897, Carl Schenck Papers, University Archives, North Carolina State University.

32. Pinchot, *Breaking New Ground*, p. 151.

33. Miller, *Gifford Pinchot and the Making of Modern Environmentalism*, p. 159-61.

34. Steen, *The U.S. Forest Service*, p. 60-64.

35. This document is reproduced in Char Miller, "Crisis Management: Challenge and Controversy in Forest Service History," *Rangelands*, June 2005, p. 14-18..

36. Miller, *Gifford Pinchot*, p. 282.

37. Hal K. Rothman, "'wA Regular Ding-Dong Fight': The Dynamics of Park-Service Controversy During the 1920s and 1930s," in Miller, ed., *American Forests*, p. 114; David A. Clary, *Timber and the Forest Service* (Lawrence: University Press of Kansas, 1986), p. 84-89.
38. Miller, *Gifford Pinchot*, p. 346-49; 351-55.
39. Miller, "Crisis Management," p. 14-18; Paul Hirt, *A Conspiracy of Optimism: Management of the National Forests Since World War Two* (Lincoln: University of Nebraska Press, 1994).

Rough Terrain
FOREST MANAGEMENT AND ITS DISCONTENTS

They came in the middle of the night, broke into Merrill Hall, site of the Center for Urban Horticulture on the campus of the University of Washington, and set incendiary devices within and around the office of researcher Terry Bradshaw; then they stole away before fiery blasts ripped through the building. The subsequent conflagration destroyed Bradshaw's facility and gutted much of the rest of the complex, causing damage estimated at $3 million. But that figure only encompassed the burned-out physical infrastructure; it has been impossible to calculate the loss of the results of decades of scientific research on such subjects as wetlands restoration, endangered plant species, urban landscaping, and genetic hybridization.[1]

It was Bradshaw's work on hybrid poplars that had been targeted for destruction. So admitted the Earth Liberation Front (ELF) in a post-fire communiqué, in which it claimed credit for the May 21, 2001, assault. Bradshaw, it asserted, is "the driving force in G.E. [genetic engineering] tree research," and was thus responsible for unleashing "mutant genes into the environment that [are] certain to cause irreversible harm to forest ecosystems." The perceived threat of his work not only sanctioned this attack, but any subsequent ones. "As long as universities continue to pursue this reckless 'science' they run the risk of suffering severe losses," ELF warned. "Our message remains clear: we are determined to stop genetic engineering."[2]

Their determination—and that of like-minded peers—had been manifest in earlier attempts to disrupt Bradshaw's research. In 1999 some of his trees were cut down as part of protests associated with that year's World Trade Organization meetings held in Seattle. Others had zeroed in on the work of Oregon State University geneticist Steve Strauss, chopping down approximately nine hundred of his hybrid poplars in March 2001; and on the same night that Merrill Hall went up in flames, ELF also torched a poplar tree farm in Clatskanie, Oregon.[3] Meanwhile, biologists at Michigan Technological University, whose research was also slated for immolation, proved more fortunate: just before dawn on November 5, 2001, campus police stumbled upon large containers of flammable liquid, complete with electrical detonators, planted outside the school's forestry building and a nearby USDA Forest Service laboratory; a police bomb squad successfully dismantled the devices.[4]

Whatever the connections between these various incidents, and whatever their outcomes—realized or foiled—it is clear that the scientific innovations associated with hybrid research and genetic engineering have escalated some people's fear of the unknown. Their anxiety is bound up with an unshakable distrust of technology and its experts, and gives shape to their worries about the emergence of a Frankensteinish world portending the end of nature. But their attacks on engineered foods and forests is not just driven by an aesthetic distaste for the manufactured and the modified, although the desire to preserve wildness owes much to late-eighteenth-century Romantic disgust with a then-industrializing world. The stakes now appear much higher, more fundamental, and thus seem to sanction more visceral reactions. As one ELF supporter wrote in the wake of the Merrill Hall fire, Bradshaw's research was "[t]ampering with the fundamental blueprint for life—the genetic code," and as such "crosses an ... ominous threshold." So threatening was this prospect that only "[s]wift and decisive action" by "dedicated Earth warriors" could halt these "emerging technological menaces before they escape the lab"; only late-night incendiarism would "protect this beautiful planet." Pacific ends, ELF and its above-ground followers insisted, justified violent means.[5]

This declaration was not unique to ELF, or even to the relatively short history of scientific forest management in the United States. Since the late-nineteenth-century importation of European ideas about how best to manage New World forests, many innovations in human ability to manipulate the forested estate have been met with doubt, suspicion, and, occasionally, violence. By tracing some of the environmental concerns, social challenges, and political controversies that have swirled around attempts to manage this well-wooded land, we will gain a better understanding of the conflicted context in which genetic engineering has emerged in the early twenty-first century.

The 1870s were a turning point in the development of a new perception of how Americans might better live on and within the land. One of the seminal texts that helped them redefine their place in nature was George Perkins Marsh's *Man and Nature: The Earth as Modified by Human Action* (1864), a shrewd analysis of the environmental devastation that the Industrial Revolution had unleashed, and a clarion call for a new conservative stewardship that would protect the Earth from human excess.[6]

Marsh warned of a coming apocalypse that could only be held off by a shift in attitude and behavior in the United States. Some who heeded his prophetic words founded the American Forest Association (1875), read widely in the European literature that Marsh himself had depended on to make his case, visited and studied with British, French, and German foresters to determine if their conceptions could be transferred across the Atlantic, and began to publish their findings in *Garden & Forest*, a new periodical devoted to the cause of conservation.

Out of this initial intellectual energy came a small bureaucratic breakthrough—the opening of the Division of Forestry in the Department of Agriculture—and a series of legislative initiatives to create national forest reserves, which finally bore fruit in 1891. Shortly thereafter, the profession of forestry surged into being, with the creation of a clutch of forestry schools, the launching of the Society of American Foresters, and the publication of the *Journal of Forestry*. By 1905, national forests, totaling more than 85 million acres, had been carved out of the public domain. A new agency, the USDA Forest Service, was founded that year with the mission of managing these forests and regulating their resources.

None of these changes could have occurred without the simultaneous transformation of the nation-state itself. Indeed, the implementation of forestry principles on the ground depended on what Bernhard Fernow, third chief of the Division of Forestry, had argued was the essential creation of a paternal government whose power trumped local rights and governance. That preeminence was precisely what Fernow's successor, Gifford Pinchot, pursued when, after President Theodore Roosevelt had tapped him to be the first chief of the new Forest Service, he hired forest rangers to patrol the vast lands under the agency's control, and fought (and won) in the courts for the rangers' right to enforce user fees for grazing, mining, and lumbering. In sanctioning these actions, the U.S. Supreme Court extended the federal government's sovereignty and legitimized a new politics of conservation, the slogan of which Pinchot coined as "the greatest good of the greatest number in the long run."[7]

Not everyone accepted this as the prevailing definition, let alone ceded to the Forest Service's exclusive assumption of professional expertise, scientific legitimacy, and political authority. Throughout the West, site of all the then-extant national forests, ranchers, miners, and timber-cutters rose up in opposition to the agency's implementation of federal conservationism. Some took the law into their own hands—violence flared, as forest rangers were shot at, beaten, or threatened with lynching when they attempted to uphold national forest boundaries or to tax resource use.[8]

The political arena was only slightly more restrained. To bolster their position, enraged westerners championed states rights as the only means to blunt what they perceived to be an aggressive executive branch; they branded its enforcement actions as "Pinchotism." One of many moments in which they came together to rail against the Roosevelt administration's actions was the 1907 Denver Public Lands Convention; the mid-June confab attracted an estimated four thousand delegates from across the West, and its raucous proceedings underscored Western frustration with the new conservation ethos.[9]

Upset that the federal government was expanding the size and number of national forests over the West's repeated protests, those at the Denver gathering demanded a showdown to determine whether the states or the executive branch held ultimate sovereignty over public lands. A Colorado newspaper denounced the arbitrary character of the Roosevelt-Pinchot edicts this way: "Very few of the autocratic monarchs of the world," the *Steamboat Pilot* asserted, "would so dare to set aside the will of the people this way." The *Rocky Mountain News* published a mocking cartoon that depicted Pinchot as a throne-sitting, mace-wielding czar; behind him were six mounted Cossacks—that is, forest rangers—brandishing whips, markers of unchecked authority. In the foreground kneel abject Westerners, hats in hand; deferential and impotent, they are no longer masters of their own fates.[10]

To defuse the charged atmosphere, Roosevelt sent Pinchot to the Denver convention, but from the start his work there was troubled: in the two days before he spoke, anti-government rhetoric built up as each of those addressing the crowd fed off his predecessor's animosity; speech after speech excoriated the Roosevelt administration and its conservation agenda. "We cannot remain barbarians to save timber," boomed Senator Henry Teller of Colorado. "I do not contend that the government has the right to seize land, but I do contend that we have the right to put it to the use that Almighty God intended."[11]

His contentious language emboldened the audience, so that when Pinchot finally strode across the stage of Denver's Brown Theater the place erupted in a vociferous round of catcalls and jeers. Hoping to deflect the hecklers' anger with a joke—"If you fellows can stand me, I can stand you,"— Pinchot gave little ground. The cornerstone of his address was what he identified as the critical relationship between national forests, conservation practices, economic growth, and political equity. "[G]overnment-regulated timber auctions prevented monopoly and the consequent excessive price of lumber," they stabilized markets and insured that there was "no question of favoritism or graft." The environmental benefits were no less important: forested lands protected "watersheds of streams used for irrigation, for domestic water and manufacturing supply, and for transportation." For these reasons alone, he asserted, "the protection of irrigation throughout the west would justify the president's forest policy."[12]

It was further justified by the fact that federal conservation took local needs into account. Grazing, for example, "is primarily a local issue and should always be dealt with on local grounds," Pinchot noted "Wise administration of grazing in the reserves is impossible under general rules based upon theoretical considerations." Being sensitive to different landscapes—natural and political—meant that "[l]ocal rules must be framed to meet local conditions, and they must be modified from time to time as local needs may require."[13]

Citizen participation in defining the mission of the national reserves also constrained federal power. In a 1907 Department of Agriculture pamphlet released to coincide with the contentious Denver meetings, Pinchot declared that public lands "exist to-day because the people want them. To make them accomplish the most good the people themselves must make clear how they want them run." But no interest, individual or combined, could or would be allowed to dominate Forest Service policy. "There are many great interests on the National Forests," and of necessity these "sometimes will conflict a little." To secure the necessary consensus that will insure a rational use of the land it "is often necessary for one man to give way a little here, another a little there." In this new Rooseveltian age, there "must be hearty cooperation from everyone."[14]

Natural forces would compel their cooperation in any event, he believed, for the carrying capacity of the land was the first and final arbiter of how and when a landscape would be utilized. "The protection of the forest and the protection of the range by wise use," Pinchot reminded his Denver audience, "are two divisions of a problem vastly larger and more important than either." This is "the problem of the conservation of all our natural resources," for if "we destroy them, no amount of success in any other direction will keep us prosperous." Private, short-term interests must give way to public, long-term needs.[15]

Many of Pinchot's listeners were not persuaded by his assertions, and Western resistance to the imposition of federal conservationism continued long after he left the Forest Service in 1910. These eruptions have been dubbed Sagebrush Rebellions, and each has been characterized by efforts to disrupt the Forest Service's capacity to manage the national forests, or to dismantle the national forest system outright.

In the 1920s, for example, Secretary of the Interior Albert Fall, a New Mexico rancher who chafed at federal grazing regulations, failed in his attempt to transfer the Forest Service (and its woods) to his department; critics believed Fall was attempting to strip the agency of its regulatory authority and perhaps sell off some of its prime lands. Similar worries surfaced in subsequent decades, pitting states rights against federal sovereignty, placed ranchers in opposition to conservationists, and framed the struggle as one between economic development and environmental preservation.[16]

That debate erupted again thirty years later. Almost single-handedly, historian and author Bernard DeVoto through his popular columns in *Harper's* fought back against the power that the Western livestock industry wielded in Congress to attack federal land-management agencies and their conservation practices. He called out the region's politicians for their alliances with those who wanted to ransack the land or appropriate it for their own ends and their use of public hearings to deliberately polarize public debate. And he stoked his readers' anger by reprinting scandalous mimeographs that had been passed among ranchers and their political minions that contained implied threats to Forest Service and its employees, such as this gem:

> The Forest Service is a child of Congress, grown up without parental discipline or instruction, an arrogant, bigoted, tyrannical off-spring, the same as any off-spring reared in the same manner, void of respect of law or customs of our land or the rights and feelings of other people.
>
> We now demand the Congress to accept the responsibility of this outrageous off-spring and put the restraining hand of parenthood to guiding it in the straight and narrow way before it runs afoul of some sterner justice.

When DeVoto concluded that these dark forces "have reversed most of the policy, weakened all of it, and opened the way to complete destruction," he wrote in language that drew off of what amounted to a half-century legacy of political tension.[17]

That contested heritage reemerged in the 1980s through what came to be called the Wise Use movement: encouraged by President Ronald Reagan's anti-environmentalism and his rhetorical assaults upon government regulation, and goaded by right-wing, vitriolic talk-radio commentators, the movement tried to assert local control over federal land. In Nevada, county commissioners crashed bulldozers through Forest Service fences in a failed attempt to lay claim to the disputed terrain. In other parts of the interior West, ranger district offices were fire-bombed and agency equipment vandalized, and, in at least one incident, a ranger discovered a pipe-bomb under his truck parked in the driveway of his home. This pattern has continued: in Utah in 2009-10, county commissioners asserted their sovereignty over unmaintained trails that wind across federal lands, ripping down Bureau of Land Management road signs; in March 2010, the state legislature and the governor even authorized the use of eminent domain to seize federal property. These long-standing battles, however much tied to the particularities of time and place, were also part of an enduring pattern of Western political protest, a pattern with which Progressive Era conservationists such as Theodore Roosevelt and Gifford Pinchot had had considerable experience.[18]

Other controversies over land management would have been less recognizable to those who had established conservationism as a key element in the American political landscape. Those who earlier had founded the major conservation agencies in the Departments of Agriculture and Interior—among them the Forest Service, National Park Service, Fish & Wildlife Service—could not have anticipated the escalating resource demands associated with the post-World War Two economic boom, or the range of political responses these changes generated.

With the close of war came an upsurge in spending on consumer items, most notably homes and automobiles. The rapid construction of new housing stock on the urban fringe and the laying down of high-speed expressways to connect these suburban developments with the metropolitan economy sparked a swift shift in timber-cutting practices. During the Great Depression of the 1930s, there had been little pressure to harvest large quantities of wood from public or private forests. Global conflict and later peace-time development changed that situation, leading the federal government and industry to initiate clearcutting practices on their respective woodlands. Systemwide production on national forests soared from 3 billion board feet (BBF) in 1945 to nearly 12 BBF in the late

1960s; in the same time period, on national forests located in the Pacific Northwest, harvests went from less than 2 BBF to 5 BBF.[19]

The houses these escalating cuts built sheltered the baby boom generation, whose parents took their numerous children on vacation to the American Wonderlands—the stunning national parks and forests. There, they encountered some of the costs associated with the suburban landscape they lived within: once-spectacular forested vistas marred by clearcuts; streams and rivers muddied; steep-sloped canyons eroded. They also confronted reminders of the world they temporarily had left behind: lines of automobiles snaked along mountain roads and packed valley parking lots, and crowds of people queued up for lodging, restaurants, and other amenities. The motoring masses brought the city to the wilderness.[20]

The inescapable tension between the desires for economic growth and open space escalated in the 1950s and 1960s, one consequence of which was that the federal land-management agencies found themselves confronted with a newly energized environmental movement that challenged prevailing scientific assurances that accelerated resource production would not damage forest and land health, and generated an ever-more intense level of public scrutiny of the agencies' failure to protect treasured landmarks. Organizations such as the Sierra Club, Wilderness Society, and National Resource Defense Council funded lawsuits that stopped the damming of some free-flowing western rivers and halted some clearcutting of both eastern and western forests; they also successfully lobbied for legislative initiatives to protect wilderness and endangered species, promote clean air and water, and sustain riparian and wetland habitats. When these political victories and congressional legislation were combined with a clutch of favorable legal mandates and a newfound expertise based on the ecological sciences, the postwar environmental movement swelled in size, political power, and cultural significance. One marker of its stature was the creation in 1970 of what has become a global celebration: Earth Day.[21]

Within a decade, however, some environmentalists would conclude that these manifold efforts were too little, too late. They feared that the Reagan administration would roll back critical environmental legislation, were riled by the unchecked militancy of the Wise Use movement, and were dismayed that now-mainstream environmental organizations appeared incapable of countering these renewed threats to Mother Earth. Those who broke off into splinter groups such as EarthFirst! and, later, the Earth Liberation Front adopted their organizational names to signal their disaffection with what they took to be their predecessors' more anthropocentric agendas; their tactics in turn were (and are) designed to shock, bloody, and disrupt those forces arrayed against what they define as planetary health and survival.

Taking their early cues from Edward Abbey's novel, *The Monkey Wrench Gang* (1975), in which fictional activists pulled up survey stakes for highway construction, disabled road-building machinery and timber-cutting equipment, and unfurled a large banner simulating a crack in the Glen Canyon Dam, real-life protesters followed suit. In time, they have graduated to potentially more deadly forms of sabotage (spiking trees slated for harvest) and more destructive forms of property damage (firebombing scientific laboratories). This escalation was signaled in 1998, when ELF incinerated three major buildings and four ski lifts in Vail, Colorado, a response to Vail, Inc.'s plans to expand into threatened lynx habitat. To further mark its repudiation of mainstream environmental rhetoric and activism, ELF posted a photograph of the flame-engulfed mountain resort on its Web page with the following inscription: "Every Night is Earth Night!"[22]

That such language offers little room for compromise is intentional. ELF has had no interest in reaching consensus with an economic system, business culture, and scientific research agenda that it believes must be destroyed. In a January 2002 communiqué following its attack on the construction site of the University of Minnesota's Microbial and Plant Genomics Research Center, a project funded in part by the Cargill Corporation: "we are fed up with capitalists like Cargill and major universities like the U of M who have long sought to develop and refine technologies which seek to exploit and control nature to the fullest extend under the guise of progress." Setting fire to heavy equipment and a on-site trailer is described as step in ELF's wider war to bring about "the end of capitalism and the mechanization of our lives."[23]

ELF's combative stance mirrors those adopted by some Western insurgents at the turn of the twentieth century who reacted violently to what they perceived as a life-threatening imposition of federal regulatory controls on grazing, lumbering, and mining. It evokes as well the actions of ELF's more-immediate contemporaries on the radical right, who in the late 1980s and early 1990s lashed out at agents of the regulatory state they despised. Marginal though each of these groups may have been (and are), their marginality nonetheless has helped shape the broader context in which each era has debated the intersection of politics and science, social change and environmental health. Dave Foreman, founder of EarthFirst!, recognized that one role the radical left of the environmental movement has played has been "to make the Sierra Club or the Wilderness Society look moderate." Contending organizations, by whatever means they choose, inevitably define and defend themselves in relation to their ideological competitors, a dynamic that will become ever more clear as the battle over genetic engineering in the fields and forests unfolds in the twenty-first century.[24]

Notes

1. "Elusive radicals escalate attacks in nature's name," *Seattle Post-Intelligencer*, June 18, 2001.
2. Earth Liberation Front, communiqué, May 21, 2001. www.earthliberationfront. com/news/2001/01052cl.mtml
3. Ibid.
4. A. Gribbon. "Genetic Debate Sprouts Over Trees," *Washington Times*, December 3, 2001; http://asp.washtimes.com/printarticle.asp?action=print&artci leID=20011203-31938212.
5. M. Tomchick. "ELF Sets A Fire at the UW," *Eat the State*, 2001, http:// eatthestate.org/05-20/ELFSetsFire.htm; Hanfords, M. "Burning Poplars II," *EarthFirst!: The Radical Environmental Journal*, 22: 2001; http://www. earthfirstjournal.org/efj/feature.cfm?ID=121&issue=v22n2.
6. George Perkins Marsh, *Man and Nature: The Earth as Modified by Human Action* (New York: Charles Scribner, 1864).
7. Bernard E. Fernow, "Providential functions of government with special reference to natural resources," *Science*, August 30, 1895: 252-54; Gifford Pinchot, *Breaking New Ground*, fourth edition (Washington, D.C.: Island Press, 1998), 261.
8. G. Michael McCarthy, *Hour of Trial: The Conservation Conflict in Colorado and the West, 1891-1907* (Norman: University of Oklahoma Press, 1977), 177; 200-210·
9. Char Miller, *Gifford Pinchot and the Making of Modern Environmentalism* (Washington, D.C.: Island Press, 2001), 162-69.
10. *Rocky Mountain News*, September 20, 1908.
11. McCarthy, *Hour of Trial*, 221-26.
12. Pinchot speech, reprinted in *Idaho Daily Statesman*, June 21, 1907.
13. *Ibid.*
14. Gifford Pinchot, *The Use of the National Forests* (Washington, D.C.: Government Printing Office, 1907), 25.
15. Miller, *Gifford Pinchot*.
16. Harold K. Steen, *The U.S. Forest Service: A History* centennial edition, (Seattle: Forest History Society and University fo Washington Press, 2004), 148-52.

17. Bernard A. DeVoto, *The Western Paradox: A Conservation Reader*, edited by Douglas Brinkley and Patricia Nelson Limerick (New Haven, CT: Yale University Press, 2000), 74-102; Bernard DeVoto, *The Easy Chair* (Boston, MA: Houghton, Mifflin, 1955), 345.

18. Hal K. Rothman, The Greening of a Nation? Environmentalism in the U.S. Since 1945 (New York: Wadsworth Publishing, 1997), 109-25; 197-207; Wilderness Society v. Kane County (No. 08-4090: January 2011); "Salazar Lays Groundwork Utah Pilot Project To resolve Old Road Claims...," http://www.blm.gov/ut/st/en/info/newsroom/2010/july/salazar_lays_groundwork.html; last accessed December 19, 2011.

19. Paul W. Hirt, *A Conspiracy of Optimism: Management of the National Forests* (Lincoln: University of Nebraska Press, 1997).

20. Paul Sutter, *Driven Wild: How the Fight Against the Automobile Launched the Modern Wilderness Movement* (Seattle: University of Washington Press, 2002).

21. Rothman, *The Greening of a Nation?*, p. 109-25; 197-207.

22. Edward Abbey, *The Monkey Wrench Gang* (Philadelphia: Lippincott, 1975); http://www.earthliberationfront.com/doa.

23. Earth Liberation Front, Communiqué, January 26, 2002: http://www.earthliberationfront.com/news/2002/020126c1; Seth Parson, "Understanding the Ideology of the Earth Liberation Front," Green Theory & Praxis: The Journal of Ecopedagogy, 4:2 (2008), 50-66, http://greentheoryandpraxis.org/journal/index.php/journal/article/viewFile/50/47, last accessed December 19, 2011.

24. Michael Parfit, "Earth First!ers wield a mean monkey wrench," *Smithsonian*, April 1, 1990, 184-204.

A Transformative Place
GREY TOWERS AND THE EVOLUTION
OF AMERICAN CONSERVATIONISM

On a beautiful late September day, just two months before he was assassinated, President John F. Kennedy spoke from the front porch of Grey Towers, the Milford, Pennsylvania, estate of Gifford Pinchot, founding chief of the USDA Forest Service. His visit served two purposes. It kicked off the president's five-day, eleven-state "conservation tour," during which he would deliver a series of addresses on the environment to buttress his conservationist credentials in a society shaken by the searing images of a poisoned nature depicted in Rachel Carson's seminal *Silent Spring* (1962). His presence in Milford also marked the Pinchot family's gift of Grey Towers to the nation, and the establishment there of the Pinchot Institute for Conservation Studies. "By its nature," Kennedy assured the large and boisterous crowd, the Institute "looks to the future not to the past. And the fact of the matter is that [it] is needed ... more today than ever before, because we are reaching the limits of our fundamental need of water to drink, of fresh air to breathe, of open space to enjoy, of abundant sources of energy to make life easier."[1]

Although the president did not know it, his dedication of Grey Towers as a critical site for the dissemination of conservation education in America—a task it has carried on since 1963—was in keeping with an earlier dedicatory moment held at the estate, this time on August 11, 1886, Gifford Pinchot's twenty-first birthday. The family selected that date to celebrate the completion of Grey Towers, their summer home, and did so in a manner that signaled their escalating focus on conservation. One sign of this was the birthday present they purchased for their oldest child, Gifford, and that was given to him by his younger brother Amos—a gilt-edged copy of George Perkins Marsh's book, *Man and Nature* (1864); this was the key nineteenth-century text warning humanity that it must adopt a comprehensive principles of land stewardship if it hoped to survive.[2] Marsh's argument had a powerful impact on those, like the Pinchots, who were profiting from the early stages of the American Industrial Revolution. Putting word to action, the senior Pinchots had committed themselves to repairing the denuded hillside on which their home had been constructed, planting trees and laying out gardens. As Gifford advised his mother several months earlier: "there are already enough trees planted on the place to take away any feeling of bleakness." Land restoration has continued at Grey Towers, such that its once logged-over and badly eroded terrain has been replaced by magnificent forest cover, an enduring testimony to the Pinchot family's long-standing conservationist ethos.[3]

Now an official national historic site, the physical structure of Grey Towers is laden with symbolism. Designed by Richard Morris Hunt and built in the robust style of a French country chateau, the mansion recalls the Pinchot family's French heritage, and their unflagging loyalty to Napoleon that resulted in their exile to America. The Marquis de Lafayette still has an honored place at Grey Towers, where his bust occupies a niche on the outside of the building, facing east toward La Belle France. Inside stands a seven-foot bronze statue of Napoleon himself, created for James Pinchot by the renowned nineteenth-century sculptor Launt Thompson, which is on long-term loan to Grey Towers from the Smithsonian Institution.

After Napoleon's final defeat at Waterloo, members of the Pinchot family, including Gifford's great-grandfather and grandfather, fled to the New World, arriving in the French Huguenot community of Milford in 1816. In part they built their fortune through the lumber business. Using practices typical of the period, these first two generations purchased tracts of forest land in eastern Pennsylvania, stripped them of merchantable timber, and rafted the logs down the Delaware River, selling them in Easton, Lumberville, and New Hope, Trenton and Philadelphia. James Pinchot later recognized the impact that such practices had had on the region, and it was through his reading of Marsh's *Man and Nature*, and its account of Mediterranean deforestation, that he understood their potential consequences on his native land. Rehabilitating Grey Towers was a local corrective, but more significant was educating Gifford to make conservation his life's work so that he could extend Marsh's precepts, and Grey Towers' example, to the nation.

While at Yale, and at his father's urging, Gifford had begun to consider forestry as a possible career, but because the profession did not exist in the United States, Pinchot went to Europe in October 1889, following graduation. Studying at L'Ecole nationale forestière in Nancy, France, and working with famed German forester, Dietrich Brandis, he returned home a year later full of evangelical zeal for sustainable forest management. He demonstrated its principles first on private forests such as George Vanderbilt's Biltmore estate in western North Carolina. He then went public with his activism when, in 1898, he was tapped as the fourth head of the Division of Forestry in the Department of Agriculture; over the next seven years, he set in motion the creation of a full-fledged national forest system under the management of the Forest Service.[4]

Although much is made of Gifford Pinchot's role in introducing "scientific forestry" from Europe to the United States, his greatest contribution to conservationism was his genius for organization: articulating a compelling and persuasive vision of the future, and inspiring people to apply their diversity of talents and energy to fulfilling that vision, he helped establish a range of institutions needed to educate foresters (the Yale Forest School, 1900); promote cooperation and professional development (the Society of American Foresters, 1900); and to hire those well-trained foresters (the Forest Service, 1905). Each of these organizations, in different ways, demonstrated the value of sustainable forest management of the nation's woodlands, public and private; influenced the development of the scientific knowledge necessary for good forest management; and disseminated vital information to communities, governmental forestry agencies, and private landowners. This innovative and interlocking network of ideas and institutions, of law, politics, and policy, stands as Gifford Pinchot's most important legacy.

Consider his role in the Transfer Act of 1905 (16 U.S.C. 472), which shifted jurisdiction over the federal forest reserves from the U. S. Department of Interior to the U. S. Department of Agriculture, a move without which there would have been no Forest Service or national forests. To bring about this much-desired end, Pinchot became involved in complex negotiations within the executive and legislative branches from the moment he was hired in 1898. The final push, supported fully by President Theodore Roosevelt, occurred in January 1905, when the president hosted the American Forest Congress, an event Pinchot largely underwrote and scripted to demonstrate to Congress the broad-based public and professional support for his ideas; the conferees came from local, state, and national governments, including commercial timber, mining, grazing, and irrigation interests, as well as conservation activists. The combination of White House pressure and intense media attention led to congressional support for the Transfer Act; its passage transformed the executive branch, insured long-term forest management on federal lands, and reflected, once more, Pinchot's political acumen and organizational skills.

During these hectic early years of his fight for conservation, Pinchot often returned to his family retreat at Grey Towers; along the Sawkill River, which flowed through the property, the ardent angler fished to his heart's content, as he would throughout his life. Hikes through its woods and engaged conversations indoors and out with family, friends, and colleagues re-energized Pinchot after long months devoted to Washington's legislative politics and bureaucratic maneuverings. Grey Towers proved even more essential during his tumultuous years as chief of the Forest Service, particularly during the grueling Ballinger-Pinchot controversy that erupted in 1909, when Pinchot challenged Interior Secretary Richard Ballinger over a sweetheart deal involving the virtual giveaway of some federal coal reserves on public lands in Alaska. The brawl turned ugly and became such a *cause célèbre* that President William Howard Taft eventually fired Pinchot for insubordination, a public martyrdom that firmly established him as a national leader in the ongoing struggle for conservation.[5]

As a private citizen, Pinchot divided his time between his home in Washington, D.C., and Grey Towers, and continued to play a prominent role in environmental debates through the National Conservation Association, which he had founded while embroiled in the grueling battle with Ballinger. Pinchot and his wife, Cornelia, made Grey Towers their permanent home in 1919, so that he could enter Pennsylvania's electoral politics. He served as the commonwealth's commissioner of forestry, was governor for two terms, and as chief executive passed legislation protecting watersheds and water quality, among a series of environmental regulations. He also ran repeatedly, if unsuccessfully, for the U.S. Senate. Pinchot never lost touch with national conservation issues, and until his death in 1946, Grey Towers was the scene of innumerable discussions and debates over natural-resource policy, involving many of the leading conservation thinkers and activists of the time.

And it was at this Milford manse, beginning in the 1920s, that he and his staff gathered together the vast trove of documents and voluminous correspondence associated with his extensive career in forestry and politics, and housed them in the Letter Box, a free-standing building on the Grey Towers grounds that functioned as a library and office during Pinchot's tenure as governor. These extraordinary records, which upon Pinchot's death were donated to the American people and relocated in the Library of Congress, became the documentary evidence on which was based his posthumously published autobiography, *Breaking New Ground*. As the introduction to its fourth edition notes, the book captures Pinchot's continuing relevance: "That more than fifty years after his death we continue to wrestle with his ideas about the meaning of conservation ... would please him no end. But he would not have been surprised," for *Breaking New Ground* was written to "convey his concerns about how best to balance the preservation and use of our natural resources, and he recognized that this issue would be central to the political debates of the future."[6]

The close attention Pinchot paid to nurturing the varied institutional, legal, and policy frameworks through which conservation can be accomplished on the ground continues at Grey Towers today, thanks to the generosity—and the vision—of subsequent generations of his family. Recognizing the iconic importance of Grey Towers to the history of conservation in the United States, Gifford Bryce Pinchot, the only child of Gifford and Cornelia Pinchot, donated the mansion and 100 acres of surrounding woodland to the public, to be administered by the Forest Service as Grey Towers National Historic Landmark. But the family did not intend Grey Towers simply to be a memorial to Gifford Pinchot's lifelong activism or for it to continue merely as a historic house museum; instead it was to serve the conservationist cause so closely associated with the family's name. Its retreat-like setting, grandson Peter Pinchot avowed, has been the perfect venue for "convening deep, contemplative discussions about how we can bring our modern civilization into balance with the rest of nature."[7]

The need to resolve this particular and crucial environmental concern has accelerated since the mid-twentieth century, due to the rapid and fundamental changes that have confronted the United States since the Pinchot Institute of Conservation was launched in 1963. The environmental worries that *Silent Spring* touched off nationally found local expression downstream of Grey Towers when citizens halted the proposed Tocks Island Dam on the Delaware River because of potential environmental impacts, setting the stage for the passage of the National Environmental Policy Act (42 U.S.C. 4321) a few years later. It was in the mid-1960s, too, that the Wilderness Act was being debated in Congress and throughout the nation, an act that became law in 1964; and the Forest Service was being buffeted by the first rumbles of public concern over the effects of commercial timber harvesting on other national forest resources. None other than Gifford Bryce Pinchot, a founding director of the National Resources Defense Council, helped ignite the intense argument over agency land management when, in 1972, after touring a clearcut in Montana's Bitterroot Valley, he decried in the name of his father the Forest Service's actions.[8]

President Kennedy did not live to see these changes emerge full blown, but he gave them inchoate expression in his 1963 dedication speech at

Grey Towers, when he urged his listeners to act as Gifford Pinchot and his generation had done, to save pristine seashores, clean up rivers, harbors, and lakes, and scrub the air clean. "I think there is evidence," Kennedy asserted, that "the nation can take action, action for which those who come after us will be grateful, which will convert killers and spoilers into allies." Since then, the bewildering array of challenges facing scientists, policymakers, and activists have only become more tangled, and the need to rise above partisan sniping and political gridlock more pressing. Meeting that challenge from the start has been part of the Pinchot Institute's mission, allowing it to play a unique role in setting conservation policy—regional, national, and international. Through technical analysis and research, the institute has provided legislators, resource professionals, and concerned citizens with data that will lead to more informed and sustainable resolutions of environmental problems; through workshops and conferences—often held at Grey Towers—it has pulled together a full range and diversity of perspectives to probe vital issues in land-use management.[9]

This integrative approach shaped the institute's first conference, held in 1965. The question it addressed—"What Needs Doing in Conservation Education During the Next Decade?"—was as ambitious as its focus, which institute director Matthew J. Brennan defined as the "'P' problems ... people, population, pesticides, pollution, and poverty." Bringing together policymakers, teachers, and curriculum specialists, this conference encouraged the construction of a more interdisciplinary program of environmental studies in schools and universities that would blend the natural sciences with social sciences and the humanities. "Only a very few of man's conservation decisions are made [solely] on the basis of scientific knowledge," Brennan argued; most are "socially desirable, politically expedient, economically feasible, or aesthetically pleasing."[10]

Determining how these varied factors have shaped our understanding of land management was at the core of a 1990 institute-sponsored workshop, which attracted writers, scientists, philosophers and theologians, lobbyists, foresters and farmers, and out of which emerged the Grey Towers Protocols, which contained a series of interlocking provisions for enhancing the conservation of public lands:

> 1. Land stewardship must be more than good "scientific management"; it must be a moral imperative.
> 2. Management activities must be within the physical and biological capabilities of the land, based upon comprehensive, up-to-date resource

information and a thorough scientific understanding of the ecosystem's functioning and response.

3. The intent of management, as well as monitoring and reporting, should be making progress toward desired future resource conditions, not on achieving specific near-term resource output targets.

4. Stewardship means passing the land and resources, including intact, functioning forest ecosystems, to the next generation in better condition than they were found.[11]

Since that conference, the Pinchot Institute has applied the moral imperatives and intellectual precepts embedded in the Grey Towers Protocols to its work on forest-certification pilot projects on corporate, tribal, and public lands. Its staff has shaped as well its analyses of "regulatory takings" as a key factor in natural-resource management; framed the results of the institute's comprehensive two-year study so that it that lays out strategies for how to achieve greater sustainability on the nation's woodlands; and its assessment of stewardship on the national wilderness preservation system. The Pinchot Institute's research agenda also has had some local consequences. Initiating land stewardship principles on lands around Grey Towers through the Milford Experimental Forest, for example, has led to research in forest ecology and sustainable forest management that serves as a model for private- and public-land managers in the Delaware Highlands and Pocono Plateau. Its assessment of the science and technology employed in the application of hydraulic fracturing on the Marcellus Shale Formation in northeastern Pennsylvania has helped frame the debate over that controversial gas-drilling process.[12]

From this work, too, has come an important international experiment in community forestry. When David Smith, who had worked on deer-management initiatives in the Milford Experimental Forest, joined the Peace Corps and was assigned to northwestern Ecuador, he sought the Pinchot Institution's collaboration on a local forestry project he conceived for the northern coastal plain of Ecuador. The institute joined with the U. S. Peace Corps, the USDA Forest Service, and Fundacíon Jutan Sacha, the largest non-governmental conservation organization in Ecuador, to work with rural communities to "sustain forestlands in that region and spark economic development." Establishing a pilot program in Cristobol Colon, a community of three hundred families owning more than 100,000 acres, the partners are working on forest management, agroforestry, wood-product development, marketing, and business management; the program's "ultimate goal is to help reverse the loss of forests in this region by providing the communities with the tools and skills to build a viable local economy based on sustainable management of their working forests." The pilot program since has grown into a full-scale initiative that is being transplanted across the region.[13]

Through these manifold examples of the institute's creative responses to the ever-evolving character of contemporary environmental dilemmas, Grey Towers National Historic Landmark has confirmed its resilience. Its claim of relevance, when set within the context of its 120-year existence, is all the more impressive: there has been no house, not even Aldo Leopold's "Shack," that has been more closely associated with the broad sweep of the history American environmental activism. That is one reason why Forest Service Chief Dale Bosworth indicated in his speech at the August 2001 rededication of the site, after a badly needed $10 million rehabilitation of its main building, that "Grey Towers is more than a piece of our national heritage. It is also a piece of our future."[14]

By working to define, and redefine, that future, Grey Towers and the Pinchot Institute will continue to respond to a critical challenge from the past that President Kennedy identified when he spoke at Milford in September 1963: "I hope that in the years to come that these years in which we live and now hold responsibility will also be regarded as years of accomplishment in maintaining and expanding the resources of our country which belong to all of our people, not merely those who are now alive but all those who are coming later." History, the president implored, will press us forward: "what Gifford Pinchot and Theodore Roosevelt and Franklin Roosevelt and Amos Pinchot, and others did in the first fifty years of this century, will serve as a stimulus to all of us in the last fifty years to make this country we love more beautiful."[15]

Notes

1. Remarks of President Kennedy at Pinchot Institute for Conservation, September 24, 1963. Grey Towers National Historic Site Collection.
2. George Perkins Marsh, *Man and Nature: The Earth as Modified by Human Action* (New York: Charles Scribner, 1864).
3. Char Miller, *Gifford Pinchot and the Making of Modern Environmentalism* (Washington, D.C.: Island Press, 2001), 55-57; Gifford Pinchot to Mary Eno Pinchot, April 27, 1886. Gifford Pinchot Papers, Library of Congress.
4. Gifford Pinchot, *Biltmore Forest: An Account of Its Treatment, and the Results of the First Year's Work* (Chicago: R. R. Donnelley and Sons, 1893).

5. Gifford Pinchot, *Fishing Talk* (Harrisburg, PA: Stackpole Books, 1993).
6. Gifford Pinchot, *Breaking New Ground* fourth edition (Washington, D.C.: Island Press, 1993), p. xi.
7. "Renovation of National Historic Landmark: Grey Towers is rededicated," pres release, Northeastern area, USDA Forest Service, August 2002.
8. Miller, *Gifford Pinchot*, p. 357-61.
9. Kennedy, "Remarks," Grey Towers NHS Collection.
10. Michael J. Brennan, "The Pinchot Institute for Conservation Studies," *Journal of Forestry*, 63(8), August 1965, 601-2.
11. V. Alaric Sample, *Land Stewardship in a Next Era of Conservation* (Milford, PA: Grey Towers Press, 1991).
12. "Evolving Toward Sustainable Forestry: Assessing Change in U.S. Forestry Organizations" (Washington, D.C.: Pinchot Institute, 1997); "Regulatory Takings: A Historical Overview and Legal Analysis for Natural Resource Management" (Washington, D.C.: Pinchot Institute, 1997); "Ensuring the Stewardship of the National Wilderness Preservation System" (Washington, D.C.: Pinchot Institute, 2001); for the institute's Marcellus Shale report, see http://www.pinchot.org/articles/335; last accessed June 17, 2011.
13. "Tropical Sustainable Forestry: A New Community Forestry Program in Northwestern Ecuador," *Pinchot letter*, 8:1, Fall 2003, 1-4; Peter Pinchot, "Demonstrating Sustainable Community Forestry in Ecuador," *Pinchot Letter*, 15:3, Fall 2010, 1, 3-10; Ariel Pinchot, "Connecting Human Health and Forest Conservation in the Rio Verde Canandé Watershed," *Pinchot Letter*, 15: 3, Fall 2010, 10-11; "Ecomadera: Market Strategies for Sustainable Forestry," http://www.pinchot.org/gp/Ecomadera; last accessed June 17, 2011.
14. Cited in "Renovation of National Historic Landmark," USDA Forest Service press release, August 2002.
15. Remarks of President Kennedy, September 24, 1963.

Thinking Like a Conservationist

Humpty Dumpty was as perplexing as anything Alice encountered when she melted through the looking glass. Their conversation, although riddled with playful double entendres, was also immensely frustrating for the young girl, who did not always understand what the prickly and precariously perched character meant by the words he uttered. When he said, for instance, that he preferred "un-birthday presents" to birthday presents (for "there are three hundred and sixty-four days when you might get un-birthday presents ... And only *one* for birthday presents"), he concluded grumpily: "There's glory for you!" Confused by this seeming non sequitur, Alice replied: "I don't know what you mean by 'glory.'" With a smile of contempt, Humpty Dumpty shot back: "Of course you don't—till I tell you. I meant 'there's a nice knock-down argument for you!'" When a puzzled Alice objected that "'glory' doesn't mean a "nice knock-down argument,'" Humpty Dumpty replied: "When *I* use a word ... it means just what I choose it to mean— neither more nor less."[1]

Humpty Dumpty has a point, and nowhere is this more amply confirmed than in the modern applications of a word so dear to the hearts of land-management professionals: conservation. As applied to the names of various contemporary federal, state, and local organizations, it has an elasticity Lewis Carroll's egg-like creation would have admired. The once-named Texas Natural Resource Conservation Commission, for example, had as its goal "clean air, clean water, and safe management of waste"; and as its mission, the protection of the Lone Star State's "human and natural resources consistent with sustainable economic development." Its counterpart in the Empire State, the New York Department of Environmental Conservation, embraces an even broader mandate and more varied responsibilities. Its turf ranges from the management of open space and outdoor recreation to the regulation of the vast bodies of water, notably the Great Lakes and the Hudson River; from monitoring the state's fish, wildlife, and marine species to licensing those who would hunt or trap them. In Maine, the Department of Conservation is similarly flexible in terms of its administrative focus. It oversees "the management, development, and protection of some of Maine's most special places," including 17 million acres of forest, 10 million acres of "unorganized territory, 47 parks and historical sites and more than 480,000 acres of public reserved land";

through its promotion of "balanced use of Maine's land, forest, water, and mineral resources," the Maine DOC hopes to benefit the state's citizens, landowners, and users.[2]

In these disparate cases, the word conservation is used to identify and reflect these agencies' attempts—whatever their success—to balance economic development with environmental protection. Striking a similar balance is perhaps more difficult to maintain for those organizations with a more explicit, resource-exploitative agenda. The mission statement of the Nebraska Oil and Gas Conservation Commission, whose motto is "Oil Serves You Every Minute of the Day," seems at pains to link pumping to protection. While its goal is to "foster, encourage, and promote the development, production, and utilization" of the state's oil and gas reserves, this must be accomplished so that their "greatest ultimate recovery" would allow "landowners, producers, and the general public [to] realize and enjoy the greatest possible good from these vital, irreplaceable natural resources." More succinct is the guiding language of the neighboring Colorado Oil and Gas Conservation Commission: "promoting the responsible development of Colorado's oil and gas."[3]

Not all conservationist organizations are squarely fixed on the development of nature's material riches. Specialists in Florida's Department of Wildlife Ecology and Conservation, a division of the state's Wildlife Extension Service, serve a critical educational function—developing programming and information that "will contribute to the solution of natural resource problems of concern to the people of Florida." The same can be said for the Conservation Education Division of the Colorado State Forest Service, which "approaches environmental education from a holistic perspective that stresses the interconnectedness of all living and non-living things." Among its programs is Project Redirect, in which some of the state's "most difficult juveniles" are set to work restoring battered landscapes as they rehabilitate themselves. This twining of environmental outcomes and social ends is also consistent with the activities of the California Conservation Corps and the Wisconsin Conservation Corps; the latter was established in 1983 "as a means to simultaneously provide employment for struggling young people and help conserve our state's valuable natural resources."[4]

One of these less-acknowledged resources is the built landscape. While the Wisconsin Conservation Corps has only begun to take on historic preservation projects, these have long been the sole emphasis of the venerable San Antonio Conservation Society. Founded in the 1920s, it has lobbied for the preservation of individual buildings, objects, urban and rural landscapes, even cultural customs, often with great success. Tourists who revel in the city's famed Riverwalk, or explore its largely intact set of eighteenth-century Spanish missions, encounter environments that this powerful organization has endeavored to protect and conserve.[5]

The concept of conservation, then, covers a lot of ground, and has always done so. As historian John Reiger has argued, George Bird Grinnell, an early champion of the idea of American conservationism, believed that "natural resources—'assets' might be a better word—must be conserved under a variety of administrative schemes. He would fight just as hard for the scientific utilization of national forests as for the preservation of natural conditions in national parks." Grinnell's ability to fuse these notions is thus consistent with the missions of modern conservation agencies that advocate the exploitation and preservation of natural resources; the utilization and restoration of landscapes; the manipulation and rehabilitation of people who work and play within rural or urban zones; the intense management of that which we call wilderness and wildlife. Yet in appearing to mean all things to all people and conditions, conservation could end up meaning nothing at all, perhaps one reason why the terms ecology and environment have become so popular in the post-World War Two era; they are thought to be more precise, less malleable.[6]

Some of this apparent imprecision and variability is a consequence of conservation's tangled linguistic origins. Entering English in the late fourteenth century, out of Latin, by way of French, conservation as an action entails what the *Oxford English Dictionary* (*OED*) denotes as the "the preservation from destructive influences, natural decay or waste" and the "preservation in being, life, health, [and] perfection." According to the OED, Chaucer is thought to have first employed the term, when in Boethius (1374) he spoke of the "conseruacioun of hyr beynge [being] and endurynge [enduring]." Two decades later, John Trevisa's 1398 translation of *Bartholomaeus Anglicus De Proprietatibus Rerum* addressed the social advantages of conservation, producing as it did "bytter thynges." This broad claim, by the mid-seventeenth century, mostly had centered on the ramifications of animal husbandry: "Rural Oeconomy," asserted essayist and poet Abraham Cowley in 1663, "would contain the Government of Bees, Swine, Poultry ... and the Domestical Conservation of and Uses of all that is brought in by Industry abroad."[7]

Conservation's early focus on the domestication of life and landscape by the late eighteenth century gained a new emphasis—it now entailed confronting, and where possible, countering threats to Nature emanating from the volatile Industrial Revolution. In response to the ever-accelerating demands for coal, iron ore, timber, and water that not incidentally scarred mountains, befouled the air, and polluted rivers and streams, individuals in Europe and later in the New World fought to protect local watersheds, wetlands, and wildlife, and advocated for the conservative development of natural resources. In the United States, as Reiger has argued, these community protests drew on European monarchical traditions of restricting access to minerals and woodlots that did not always sit well with the American populist political culture. Over time, however, Antebellum Era hunters and fishermen joined political leaders such as John Quincy Adams in recognizing that the most effective way to conserve forests and wildlife was to adopt "concepts and practices already developed in aristocratic societies on the other side of the Atlantic."[8]

Vermonter George Perkins Marsh was one of those who acted on this insight. In 1857, he wrote a ground-breaking report on the pressing need for his home state to resuscitate ailing fish populations in the Connecticut River and its many tributaries; he made explicit use of earlier European analyses of declining riparian species, and of their experiments at cleaning water courses and restocking fish grown in hatcheries. Seven years later, he followed up this argument with his remarkably prescient and influential book, *Man and Nature* (1864). Written while he served as a U.S. diplomat in Italy, where he everywhere observed humanity's deleterious impact on the Mediterranean basin, Marsh's tome was a catalyst to the development of the late-nineteenth-century American conservation movement. It "was the first book to recognize the full significance of the human species as an environmental agent," Reiger notes, "the first to realize the appalling losses caused by the destruction of natural resources, and the first to propose a remedy for the future."[9]

It is striking, therefore, that Gifford Pinchot would later assert that he had invented the idea of conservationism. Although he knew conservation's many foreign and domestic antecedents, if only because he had carefully read George Perkins Marsh's *Man and Nature*, and had been trained as a forester in Europe in some of conservation's most potent intellectual constructs, he would swear that the idea originated with him while he was on a horseback ride along Ridge Road in Washington D.C.'s Rock Creek

Park in February 1907. As chief, he often rode his horse, Jim, through this thickly wooded terrain to shake off the day's concerns. On this particular winter afternoon, however, he had taken "his problems with him ... when he meant to leave them behind." At the forefront of his mind was a vexing public-policy conundrum: how best to coordinate and manage the nation's public lands, and the people's use of them. Oversight responsibility was badly fragmented, Pinchot believed, as individual departments and bureaus jockeyed for power. "To put it in a sentence, there were three separate Government organizations which dealt with mineral resources, four or five concerned with streams, half a dozen with authority over forests, and a dozen or so with supervision over wild life, soils, soil erosion, and other questions of the land." While pondering what might bind these many, great, and jealous interests together, Pinchot claimed to have had an epiphany: "Suddenly it flashed through my head that there was a unity in this complication—that the relation of one resource to another was not the end of the story," but its commencement. What wrought order out of chaos was a belief in the power of conservation to transform human endeavor. "When the use of all the natural resources for the general good is seen to be a common policy with a common purpose," Pinchot wrote, "the chance for the wise use of each of them becomes infinitely greater than it had ever been before." This led him to believe that the "[c]onservation of natural resources is the key to the future," and to even more grandly predict it would also be "the key to the safety and prosperity of the American people, and all the people of the world, for all time to come."[10]

Pinchot's sense of the encompassing character of this vision would sharpen in time. "There was too much of it for me to take it all in at once," he admitted. "As always my mind worked slowly" and that "day in Rock Creek Park I was far from grasping the full reach and swing of the new idea." Only after extensive conversations with his colleagues in the Forest Service, and with other government scientists, most notably W. J. McGee, head of the Bureau of American Ethnology, whom Pinchot credited with distilling his idea to its essence, did he recognize its full implications. The goal of conservationism, he would write in a 1905 letter—two years before his Rock Creek Park reverie—and in language borrowed from McGee and British philosopher Jeremy Bentham, was to generate "the greatest good, for the greatest number in the long run."[11]

Even if only an adaptation or modification, Pinchot's definition of conservation was significant in two respects. His coupling of "the long run" to the utilitarian notion of "the greatest good" committed conservation to the creation of sustainable economies and ecosystems, a potentially important notion for a society so wedded to profligacy and waste. His vision of conservation also made a more narrow, albeit valuable contribution to the resolution for how competing federal land-management agencies might better cooperate.

That there are problems with this conceptualization of conservation is also clear. Who defines what the greatest good is, and on what basis? How to measure its production and equitable distribution? More confounding: how are we to weigh human material needs against environmental conditions over time? Was it not plausible, moreover, that succeeding generations would redefine what constitutes the greatest good? About the resolution of these issues, Pinchot was less voluble. What he was convinced of—and spoke frequently about—was that only a rigorous pursuit of conservation under federal leadership would enable this democratic society to provide a steady stream of goods and services to bolster the citizenry's standard of living and to deliver on its social promise. Opposed to material inequalities, respectful of the land, and determined to account for the needs of subsequent generations, Pinchot's notion of conservation seemed to promise the resolution of some of the most enduring problems confronting an industrializing America.[12]

Even acknowledging his intellectual conception of and political contributions to the definition of conservation, one also has to admire Pinchot's aggressive claim to have coined the idea. Perhaps Humpty Dumpty can best explain this bit of self aggrandizement. When Alice cast doubt on the egg-man's right to define a word's meaning, he shot back that the "question is ... which is to be master—that's all."[13]

But why give the last word to a fictional egg, especially one whose admitted goal was to confuse not clarify? There are, in short, more relevant sources than Humpty Dumpty to illuminate the larger meaning of conservation. For instance, Frank B. Gill, former president of the American Ornithological Union, in his preface to *The Birds of Ecuador: A Field Guide*, argues that true conservationists cannot separate scientific analyses from their social or political implications. That is because "conservation is born of discovery and wonder, then of understanding, and finally of action." It offers its adherents ways of appreciating and knowing nature, from which come an obligation to protect it.[14]

Although framed around the need to preserve imperiled avian life and habitat, Gill's comment resonates with ecologist Aldo Leopold's earlier, and similarly compelling, claims about the essential self-consciousness that envelopes the conservation ethos. "I have read many definitions of what is a conservationist, and written not a few myself," he observed in *Sand County Almanac* (1949), "but I suspect that the best one is not written with a pen, but with an axe. It is a matter of what a man thinks about while chopping, or while deciding what to chop." Those internal thoughts have external implications: "A conservationist is one who is humbly aware that with each stroke he is writing his signature on the face of his land." Only with that self-awareness will we be able to acknowledge that "conservation is a state of harmony between men and land"—and then live accordingly.[15]

Notes

1. Lewis Carroll, *Alice in Wonderland and Through the Looking Glass* (New York: Grosset & Dunlap, Publishers, 1983), 238-39.
2. www.tnrcc.state.tx.us/mission.html; www.dec.state.ny.us/; www.state.me.us/doc/index.html
3. www.oil-gas.state.ne.us/; www.oil-gas.state.co.us/
4. http://www.wec.ufl.edu/extension/mission.htm; http://www.colostate.edu/Depts/CSFS/csfsed.html; http://www.dwd.state.wi.us/wcc/Overview.htm
5. Lewis Fischer, *Saving San Antonio: The Precarious Preservation of a Heritage*, (Lubbock: Texas Tech University Press, 1996); Char Miller, "Salvage Crew," *Texas Observer*, February 14, 1997, p. 28-29.
6. John F. Reiger, *American Sportsmen and the Origins of Conservation*, third edition, (Corvallis: Oregon State University Press, 2001), 143; Samuel P. Hays, "From Conservation to Environment: Environmental Politics in the United States Since World War II," in Char Miller and Hal K. Rothman, eds., *Out of the Woods: Essays in Environmental History* (Pittsburgh: University of Pittsburgh Press, 1997), 101-26; Bob Pepperman Taylor, *Our Limits Transgressed: Environmental Political Thought in America* (Lawrence: University of Kansas Press, 1992).
7. *OED*: http://www.oed.com/view/Entry/39564?redirectedFrom=conservation#eid; last accessed June 20, 2011.
8. Reiger, *American Sportsmen*, 6.
9. Reiger, *American Sportsmen*, 22-23; David Lowenthal, *George Perkins Marsh: Prophet of Conservation* (Seattle: University of Washington Press, 2000), 182-85.
10. Gifford Pinchot, *Breaking New Ground*, fourth edition (Washington, D.C.: Island Press, 1998), 322-23.
11. *Ibid.*, 261.
12. *Ibid.*, p. 322-26.
13. Carroll, *Alice in Wonderland*, 238.
14. Robert S. Ridgely and Paul S. Greenfield, *The Birds of Ecuador: A Field Guide*. Foreword by Frank B. Gill (Ithaca, NY: Cornell University Press, 2001), x.
15. Aldo Leopold, *A Sand County Almanac and Sketches Here and There* (New York: Oxford University Press, 1949), 68, 207.

POLICY SCHEMES

Establishing national forests has required the enactment of legislation, writing of policy, and judicial review to insure that however these public lands would be used—for timber, grass, or recreation—that these uses are compatible with the law and the carrying capacity of the land itself. The Antiquities Act (1906) and the Weeks Act (1911), like the landmark case *United States v. Grimaud* (220 U. S. 506), are critical examples of new legal authorities that helped usher in a more powerful executive branch during the Progressive Era. But whether the management ethos of the Forest Service, born in the late nineteenth century, remains valid in the twenty-first remains contested.

Landmark Decision
THE ANTIQUITIES ACT,
BIG-STICK CONSERVATION,
AND THE MODERN STATE

Roy Neary could not help himself. At dinner, he played with his mashed potatoes. Had he been a child, no one would have much minded, but he was a father, and his wife and three children anxiously watched his meal-time antics. Ever since that fearsome night when the power was suddenly cut off, he had become ever-more reclusive and odd, so much so that at dinner the kids had scooted closer to their mother. From that remove they watched, furtively, as he molded the white mound topped with melting margarine into a small peak; and then, with ill-disguised fear, as he lunged across the table, grabbed the bowl of steaming spuds, and began ladling gob after gob on to his plate. That's when, "like a mad potter, Neary started to knead the white mush with his hands into some kind of shape," which emerged into a rough approximation of Devils Tower. That's when we know the aliens made him do it.[1]

But why did Steven Spielberg frame his sci-fi thriller, *Close Encounters of the Third Kind* (1977), around that remote Wyoming landmark? Why in a later scene have a half-crazed Neary upgrade his food-art project into a hardened nine-foot exact replica of the haunting land form; and then, after a harrowing journey, have him come face-to-face with the object of his desire before which he stood speechless: "The Tower stood alone, unique, something so one-of-a-kind that Neary felt a chill across his shoulders at the thought he was able to reproduce it in sculpture without even knowing it existed." Why that place?[2]

Perhaps for some of the same reasons that several Northern Plains tribes have been drawn to what they revere as Mateo Tipi, Bears Lodge, though they remain a good deal more vocal in their appreciation of its formidable power than was the tongue-tied Neary. The monolith has played a formative role in legends of the Arapaho and Cheyenne, Crow, Kiowa, and Sioux. Several of these, transcribed in the 1930s, used bears' claws scratching at the tower's surface to explain its deeply grooved sides. Its soaring height is said to be a consequence of the Great Spirit's lifting ground-level rocks into its present elevated form to save children from marauding bruins. Other tales explain the creation of the constellation Pleiades by evoking the plight of seven sisters, saved from earthly demise—once more at the claws of bears—by godly intervention. For the Plains peoples, Bears Lodge occupies a special dimension, a spiritual portal between this world and the other-worldly.

So it also functioned for Steven Spielberg, who concluded his film with a now-obsessed Roy Neary walking across a hastily constructed "cosmic port of call" at the tower's base and toward a massive intergalactic spacecraft. Forever alienated from his family, he does not hesitate to step into this "fiery heart of the mystery," and as its gateway closes after him, the craft lifts off into a "scaffold of light," a "brilliant stairway up to the heavens," transported into the night sky where it becomes the "brightest of the brightest stars."[3]

A divine domain, Devils Tower is also a massive, perpendicular obelisk, formed of molten rock and estimated to be more than fifty million years old, lodged within a human, that is, political environment. Designated a national monument, its use is now regulated by the National Park Service, a bureaucratic reification of legal status it gained in September 1906 when President Theodore Roosevelt signed a piece of paper absorbing it into the American polity. He did so by invoking the Antiquities Act, passed that same year, congressional legislation that granted the presidency extraordinary powers to preserve "historic landmarks, historic and prehistoric structures, and other objects of historic or scientific interest that are situated upon the lands owned or controlled by the Government of the United States." However prosaic, Roosevelt's stroke of the pen marked an iconic moment: Devils Tower became the first national monument.

The landmark's political ascension has had earth-bound consequences. Because its modern history has been linked to the Antiquities Act, an initiative emblematic of the Progressive Era in which it was crafted, Devils Tower has contributed to the development of a new form of land management in the American West, the realignment of the relative power of the executive and legislative branches of the federal government, and the implementation of a hitherto-untested preservationist ethos on a frontier landscape. Through a secular legislative act, the state, at Devils Tower and elsewhere, created a new kind of sacred space—national in name, sweep, and scope—a legacy of unparalleled significance.

To understand why Congress passed the Antiquities Act, it is essential to recognize that those who called themselves Progressives believed deeply in the capacity of government to mold the commonweal, present and future.

Sharing that faith with Roosevelt was the act's central framer, Representative John F. Lacey of Iowa, and its leading advocates, notably Edgar L. Hewett, W. H. Holmes, and the Reverend Henry Mason Baum. Emerging out of the late nineteenth century, and buffeted by while benefiting from the industrial revolution, this cohort of like-minded reformers drew heavily on European social idealism to shape their perspectives on the necessity of a strong central state. So pervasive was this trans-Atlantic transfer of ideas that historian Daniel Scott has argued it is the era's defining feature. Making this "Atlantic era in social politics" possible was the creation of a "new set of institutional connections" with European societies, and influential go-betweens or brokers who facilitated the vital traffic in intellectual commerce. This was as true for child-welfare advocates as it was for foresters, politicians as well as ethnologists; as much for Jane Addams and Gifford Pinchot as for Teddy Roosevelt and the Smithsonian's W. H. Holmes. The key to a more progressive society, they all affirmed, was the establishment of a more paternal nation state. This European import, shorn of its monarchical trappings, would be the foundation of a potent Republic.[4]

As they imagined a new society, these Progressives dreamed of a new social type—-the professional. Well trained in the relevant graduate-school programs, and bearing away hard-won knowledge and a crucial credential (the requisite terminal degree in their field), these experts would commit themselves to resolving nagging social ills, from urban poverty to rural immiseration, from political malfeasance to timber theft and relic poaching. That these seemingly disparate issues were of a piece to this generation of American reformers, many of whom received their post-graduate education in Europe or at the new U. S. universities modeled after continental norms, was critical to their progressivism, an ideal that was global in reach and local in application. Because their "talents meshed with others in a national scheme," historian Robert Wiebe has observed, this generation felt encouraged "to look outward confidently." And it was their "earnest desire to remake the world upon their private models" and professional ambitions that "testified to the deep satisfaction accompanying this revolution in identity."[5]

But the identity politics of the late nineteenth century, particularly for those of the urban middle class from which many of the Progressives came, were fraught with complications. Products of the new order they hoped to impose on what they perceived to be an unruly society and unkempt culture, they were also children of an earlier era. These sons and daughters came of age amid the tumultuous upheaval accompanying the shift from an agricultural to an industrial economy, a nation at once bucolic and citified, still torn in its grief over a brutal civil war, as uncertain about how to incorporate its newly liberated African American citizens as it would be wary in its welcome of millions of new immigrants. These divisions, sharp, ragged, and painful, animated the late-nineteenth-century political arena that nurtured progressive visions, giving visionaries cause and context for their work. Convinced that through the scientific method and bureaucratic means they would be able to reconstruct society, these young reformers had "enough insight into their lives to recognize that the old ways and old values would no longer suffice," Wiebe argues. "Often confused, they were still the ones with the determination to fight those confusions and mark a new route into the modern world." Who then did they tap to shepherd them to the promised land but a figure emblematic of Eastern aristocracy and Western rough-and-tumble: "Seeking a new urban leader for modern America, many gave their hearts to a man almost invariably pictured in a cowboy hat, Theodore Roosevelt."[6]

In retrospect, it almost seems predictable that a crusading President Roosevelt would affix his signature on the Act for the Preservation of American Antiquities (1906). As a child, he had tromped through forest and marsh in search of bird, mammal, and fish, preternaturally fascinated with the wild and its mysteries, convinced that by collecting specimens, and studying his finds, he could penetrate a fecund world beyond himself. Coming into knowledge of it, and displaying his insights, was also part of his precocious commitment to science, very much on display when at age eight he spotted a dead seal in front of a New York shop. As biographer Paul Cutright relates the tale, young Teddy was transfixed, day after day returning to the scene, measuring its length, width, and girth, recording its shape, color, and anatomy, and, in the intervals, perhaps begging his resistant parents to let him purchase the by-now-rotting corpse. If his goal had been to secure the full skeleton, he failed, but he came away with its skull, an achievement, Cutright writes, that sparked "two decisions, each of which would importantly shape his future. He determined, first, that he would become a naturalist, and, next, that he would found his own museum, using the seal skull as a nucleus."[7]

Young Teddy pursued both ventures with great success, and because of his skills as collector and taxidermist the grandly titled Roosevelt Museum of Natural History exploded in size, becoming home to thousands of expertly stuffed animals. Within five years, he made the first of his donations to New York's American Museum of Natural History (which his father helped establish), and later presented the bulk of his collection to the Smithsonian Institution, which kept hundreds of unique contributions, sending duplicate specimens to museums around the country. Long before he became the nation's twenty-sixth president, Roosevelt had demonstrated his preservationist instinct and pedagogic impulse.[8]

To save and teach: those aspirations were at the heart of the conservationist credo he began to adopt (and model) in the coming years. "His active outdoor life, as boy and man, had made him thoroughly alive to the value of timberland and its essential relation to soil, flood control, and water conservation," Cutright observes. Later, his years in the American West would offer up new lessons, "abundant opportunities to observe firsthand the rapid destruction of the buffalo, elk and other large game, and, in the more arid lands—including the barren, exposed walls of the Badlands' canyons—he ... became more deeply aware of the effects of perennial, unchecked erosion." This devastation of fauna and landform was troubling. It also brought to a climax a mythic moment. The evidence on the ground appeared to confirm for Roosevelt, and those who joined him in the Boone & Crockett Club, among other conservationist ventures, that contemporary historian Frederick Jackson Turner was correct: by 1890, the American frontier had closed.[9]

With it went the masculinized landscape of exploration and survey, contest and conquest, a rugged terrain against which Roosevelt had tested himself. There were compensations, and one of them was conservation, as an idea and an act. Framed around scientific methodologies, Hal K. Rothman avers in *Preserving Different Pasts*, conservationism "gave the nation a way to counter the anxiety created" by the disappearance of frontier and wilderness; because it "allowed for the planning for the future through goals of increased efficiency and equitable distribution," it was an antidote to this cultural unease and a prescription for a healthier body politic. Through a sustained application of this progressive balm, the nation's forests would be regenerated, its battered lands reinvigorated, and its prehistoric past reclaimed—heroic work for a modernist generation.[10]

That antiquities-advocate Edgar Hewett recognized the connections between various Progressive reform efforts is reflected in his 1904 comment—published, appropriately, in *Science*—that a "system of governmental protection of archaeological remains is manifestly an accomplished fact, as much so and after the same manner as is the protection of timber on public lands." His claim was premature; a system of protection was not yet the "accomplished fact" he proclaimed it to be, nor would it be fully realized when, two years later, the Antiquities Act became law. But the need for systematic public control of and protection for the remnants of ancient civilizations in the West was much touted in the late nineteenth century. Every subsequent retelling of the origins of the Antiquities Act, drawing on contemporary congressional testimony and journalistic exposés, recounts the increased number of thieves scouring Southwestern canyons in search of relics; describes the inability of well-meaning local and state organizations to defend these sites or to think beyond regional interests; and analyzes the emerging consensus among an Eastern elite that a national perspective, defined and enforced by federal authority, was required to stop vandals from pilfering the nation's archeological heritage.[11]

This is essentially the same narrative spun by contemporary conservationists pressing for regulation of natural resources, and, as Hewett recognized, these shared stories played to and off one another, benefiting each. There was a philosophical reason for this linkage, President Roosevelt asserted in his Fifth Annual Message to Congress in 1905. In it, he attributed the Progressive movement's ideological origins, its hunger for rational restraint, to Edmund Burke, citing his declaration that "[m]en are qualified for civil liberty in exact proportion to their disposition to put moral chains on their own appetites." This being so, the eighteenth-century political theorist had asserted, it is ordained "in the eternal constitution of things that men of intemperate minds cannot be free. Their passions forge their fetters." The Forest Service, founded as part of the Department of Agriculture six months before Roosevelt's 1905 address, and the Antiquities Act, gaining congressional sanction six months later, were in Roosevelt's mind linked together in the essential chain of self-governance.[12]

Not all shared the president's faith in Burkean principles. Critics of the Antiquities Act (and, by extension, the Forest Service) charged that Roosevelt and his Progressive allies were concentrating authority in the executive branch, hoping to make it first among equals, the driving engine of a new nation-state. They were not wrong. Whether in the Department of the Interior or Agriculture, the conservation agencies and controls they came to possess over public lands and people's behaviors began to segregate land use and users, and separate parks from forests from monuments. To challenge this system of national management and zoning in the West, contemporaries adopted a Jeffersonian retort to what they perceived to be an ominous federal imperium, unfurling the banner of state's rights.

Their political challenge has found academic favor. The federal government gained greatly from the passage of the Antiquities Act, Rothman has observed. "No piece of legislation invested more power in the presidency," and its "vaguely defined scope, encompassing 'objects of historic or scientific interest,' made it an unparalleled tool" for an expansion-minded chief executive. Consider the Act's apparent concession to congressional worries about the potential size of national monuments, captured in language stipulating that they "be confined to the smallest area compatible with the proper care and management of the objects to be protected." On January 11, 1908, Roosevelt demonstrated just how elastic that terminology could be when he declared the Grand Canyon to be a national monument, and brought within its limits more than 800,000 acres. His initiative was as well a vivid illustration of how the Act allowed him "to circumvent the fundamentally languid nature of congressional deliberation and instantaneously achieve results he believed were in the public interest." Or as Douglas Brinkley has observed: "The Antiquities Act was a dangerous precedent to set with Roosevelt in the White House. ... To think that Roosevelt wouldn't stretch his new powers to the extreme was naïve."[13]

In setting a critical precedent that many of his successors would employ, Roosevelt's use of the Antiquities Act in its own way contributed to what Arthur M. Schlesinger, Jr., and, more recently, Stephen Grauband, have denounced as the "Imperial Presidency"—for them, the origins of a chief executive freed from, and dismissive of, congressional oversight (and that later would morph into malevolent proportions under Richard M. Nixon and George W. Bush, among others) lay in Progressive-Era experimentation. Although those latter-day constitutional corrosions were not the ends TR and the Progressives had in mind, their ambitions were imperialistic. So argue Richard Nelson and Sally K. Fairfax: for them, the Age of Roosevelt the First must be understood in the context of the Spanish-American War of 1898 and the colonial possessions that in its aftermath the United States brought to heel. This overseas militarism would find domestic expression in the simultaneous demarcation of landscapes into national forests, monuments, and parks protected by uniformed civilian guards, often mounted and armed, signifiers of state power and national prerogative.

Antiquities Act preservationism thus played its part in advancing executive clout at the expense of local control.[14]

For all its compelling power, this argument can be overplayed, for its analytical force depends on a retrospective view, a critique of the excesses of Big Government that emerged in the wake of the second President Roosevelt and his liberal Democratic heirs, Harry S. Truman, John F. Kennedy, and Lyndon B. Johnson (and perhaps Barack Obama). Yet the New Deal, and the welfare state it initiated, which reached its zenith with the Great Society legislation of the 1960s, pressed well beyond Progressive-Era realities, as is manifestly evident in an examination of the impact of the Antiquities Act in its first twenty years.

To suggest that it even had an impact is, in some cases, a stretch. Begin with the letter that Gifford Pinchot, chief of the Forest Service, wrote to his forest officers nearly six months after the Act's passage. "The importance of taking steps to preserve such objects has become very apparent, and as soon as possible I wish you to report specifically upon each ruin or natural object of curiosity in your reserve, recommending for permanent reservation all that will continue to contribute to popular, historic, or scientific interest." Emphasizing that the "areas selected should be compatible with the proper care and management of the objects to be protected," and urging his staff to be mindful of the possibility of these sites "being entered under the mineral laws," the nation's forester said nothing about how these landmarks, once located, identified, and surveyed, would be managed. He had nothing to say because he had no idea what would constitute good management, and neither did his peers in the Interior Department's General Land Office (GLO), on whose lands national monuments also would be established. In this respect, they were as well informed as the president—but their collective cluelessness did not stop Theodore Roosevelt. After creating Devils Tower National Monument in September 1906, he designated seventeen additional sites, totaling more than 1.2 million acres, before he left office in March 1909.[15]

But of what consequence were these designations? Written in response to depredations at historic and sacred sites, the Antiquities Act proved powerless to defend their archeological value and cultural import. None of the first generation of national monuments witnessed sustained supervision until the 1930s, and some not even then. Agents of the GLO and Forest Service rarely visited the landmarks, their offices' already small budgets contained no line items for monument protection, and neither agency constructed a management plan that would have strengthened its sense of responsibility for these endangered properties' care. These guardians' most proactive move was to tack up signs demarcating federal property lines, an action that did not occur at Devils Tower, for example, until 1919, thirteen years after its creation as a National Monument![16]

"Warning-sign preservation," in short, did little good. "The pothunting that had preceded the Antiquities Act remained endemic at archaeological sites, and the influx of people into the Southwest after 1900 increased the potential for scavenging, digging, and callous misuse," Rothman demonstrates. Add to this thievery the casual vandalism, unauthorized hunting, and illegal grazing that occurred beyond the gaze of absentee rangers and officers, to say nothing of the "natural decay of historic and prehistoric features," and the idea of enhanced federal power emanating from Antiquities Act acquisitions becomes laughable. As Frank Bond, chief clerk of the GLO worried in 1911: "It is only a question of time when [the national monuments] will be secretly attacked and pillaged piecemeal, until there is nothing left to preserve." They are, he concluded, "a responsibility which we now feel but can not make effective."[17]

Navajo National Monument is a case study in the difficulties associated with defining the legal status of and projecting authority over an ancient religious landscape. An in-holding of the sprawling Navajo reservation in northeastern Arizona, it comprises three non-contiguous segments, separated by considerable distance. "Awkward and gerrymandered" in size and location, the monument "had no place in the thinking of the people" who delineated its boundaries. "They sought to preserve its ruins, apparently assuming that the remote nature of the monument would protect it forever." Off the map in the usual touristic sense—it lacked roads and service facilities until the 1960s—it also was beyond the ken of its governmental administrators. Navajo National Monument, Rothman concludes, "had no advocates or constituents save archaeologists, no one who could argue that it merited the attention of the federal bureaucracy."[18]

The same could be said of Shoshone Cavern in Wyoming or Montana's Lewis and Clark Cavern, Devils Postpile in California, or Utah's Mukuntuweap (now Zion National Park). Even the much-visited Grand Canyon, with regular stagecoach transit from the railhead in nearby Williams, Arizona, received little direct management and no federal investment in tourist infrastructure. Private investors, whose hotels and other service properties often encroached on that fabled landscape, were the gatekeepers to and provided interpretation of what Theodore Roosevelt had proclaimed to be the canyon's "wonderful grandeur." With the exception of those few spectacular settings that earned national park status with the advent of the National Park Service in 1916, the rest of the national monuments remained, in Rothman's words, "second-class sites," or, worse, "peripheral oddities" lost in a "system increasingly focused on scenic monumentalism."[19]

Long ignored, the monuments finally gained greater relevance during the Great Depression. President Franklin Roosevelt's New Deal initiatives, particularly the escalating appropriations funneled through the Civilian Conservation Corps, helped construct on their grounds a more tourist-friendly landscape. New trails and cabins, scenic overlooks, and visitor centers integrated the once-neglected monuments into the larger, national system of recreation; increases in staffing helped too, allowing for much-needed protection of archeological remnants and cultural resources. An ever-more centralized bureaucratic structure within the Park Service, reflective of Interior Secretary Harold Ickes' top-down management style, also enhanced the monuments' place within the National Park Service mission. But the most revolutionary change occurred as a result of Executive Order 6166. Drawn up by President Herbert Hoover and signed by Franklin Roosevelt on June 10, 1933, the EO instituted new efficiencies in federal governance. One of its mandates was the transfer to the Park Service of all non-Interior Department parks, memorials, and historic sites, as well as all the national monuments that had been created under the Antiquities Act. Included in the transfer were the ten national monuments that had been assigned to the War Department (from Cabrillo in California to Fort Matanzas in Florida), as well as the fourteen national monuments remaining under Forest Service jurisdiction (from Chiricahua on the Coronado National Forest to Wheeler on the Cochetopa & Rio Grande National Forests). By his signature, Roosevelt ensured that preservation had become the exclusive purview of the NPS. With that expanding responsibility came a widening of the agency's managerial agenda, and the institution of more formal controls over its far-flung properties; its former policy of neglect, at once benign and baleful, became a thing of the past.[20]

Despite its more muscular presence in and stronger regulation of the national monuments, the National Park Service still sought democratic ends. Access to even the most remote sites accelerated with the construction of roads and services; the agency also built over time a more astute and motivated constituency in support of its conception of preservation. This support in turn strengthened the Park Service's self-promotional claim of enhancing the nation's appreciation for America the Beautiful, and its unique status as the keeper of a civic religion framed around the West's monumental landscapes. That these sites might be woven into the cultural imagination, becoming part of a national dialogue about what made the United States exceptional, had also appealed to Theodore Roosevelt's conservationist sensibility. While standing on the South Rim of the Grand Canyon in 1903, poised to speak about the "natural wonder" that lay at his feet, the usually loquacious Roosevelt fell silent: "I shall not attempt to describe it, because I cannot. I could not choose the words that would convey or could convey to any outsider what that canyon is." But he would raise his voice in its defense. "Leave it as it is. Man cannot improve on it; not a bit. The ages have been at work on it and man can only mar it." Convinced that his fellow citizens had an obligation to protect the canyon's startling vastness, and certain that this national treasure evoked our virtue, he urged his audience to consider its preservation as a peculiarly American gift to the future: "keep it for your children and your children's children and for all who come after you."[21]

Among those who benefited from Roosevelt's plea, which, three years later, he put into legal force with the signing of the Antiquities Act, was a fictional figure. Like TR, Roy Neary projected his fantasy of democratic self-expression on to a totemic terrain, and from Devils Tower National Monument launched his quest for immortality, his reach for the stars.

Notes

1. Steven Spielberg, *Close Encounters of the Third Kind* (New York: Delacorte Press, 1977), p. 141-42.
2. *Ibid.*, p. 181-83.
3. The Plains Indians' legends are collected at http://www.nps.gov/deto/stories.htm, last accessed on January 19, 2005; Ray H. Mattison, "Devils Tower National Monument: The First Fifty Years," posted at http://www.nps.gov/deto/first50_text. htm, last accessed on January 19, 2005; Spielberg, *Close Encounters of the Third Kind*, p. 250-51.
4. Daniel T. Rodgers, *Atlantic Crossings: Social Politics in a Progressive Age* (Cambridge: The Belknap Press of Harvard University Press, 1998), p. 3-4.
5. Robert H. Wiebe, *The Search for Order, 1877-1920* (New York: Hill & Wang, 1967), p. 113; suggesting the limitations of this new identity is Eileen L. McDonagh, "Race, Class, and Gender in the Progressive Era: Restructuring State and Society," in Sidney M. Milkis and Jerome M. Mileur, eds., *Progressivism and the New Democracy* (Amherst: University of Massachusetts Press, 1999), p. 145-84.

6. Wiebe, *The Search for Order,* p. 131-32; McDonagh, "Race, Class, and Gender," p. 171-84.
7. Paul Russell Cutright, *Theodore Roosevelt: the Making of a Conservationist* (Urbana: University of Illinois Press, 1985), p. 1-2.
8. Cutright, *Theodore Roosevelt,* p. 26; 29-31; 37; 50; 70-71; 139.
9. *Ibid.,* p. 212-13; on the Boone & Crockett Club, see John Reiger, *American Sportsmen and the Origins of Conservationism,* third edition (Corvallis: Oregon State University Press, 2001).
10. Kathleen Dalton, *Theodore Roosevelt: A Strenuous Life* (New York: Alfred A. Knopf, 2002); Sarah Watts, *Rough Rider in the White House: Theodore Roosevelt and the Politics of Desire* (Chicago: University of Chicago Press, 2003); Hal Rothman, *Preserving Different Pasts: The American National Monuments* (Urbana: University of Illinois Press, 1989), p. 15-16; see also Samuel P. Hays, *Conservation and the Gospel of Efficiency: The Progressive Conservation Movement, 1890-1920* (Cambridge: Harvard University Press, 1959).
11. Ronald Freeman Lee, "The Antiquities Act of 1906," edited by Raymond Harris Thompson, *Journal of the Southwest,* 42: 2 (Summer 2000), p. 219-23; Raymond Harris Thompson, "Edgar Lee Hewett and the Political Process," *Journal of the Southwest,* 42: 2 (Summer 2000), p. 271-318; Rothman, *Preserving Different Pasts,* p. 1-30; Douglas Brinkley, *The Wilderness Warrior: Theodore Roosevelt and the Crusade for America* (New York: Harper, 2009), p. 642-49.
12. Theodore Roosevelt, Fifth Annual Message, December 5, 1905, posted at www.geocities.com/presidentialspeeches/1905htm?200522, last accessed on February 22, 2005.
13. Hal K. Rothman, "The Antiquities Act and National Monuments: A Progressive Conservation Legacy," *CRM,* 22:4, 1999, p. 16-18; Brinkley, *The Wilderness Warrior,* p. 644.
14. Arthur M. Schlesinger, Jr., *The Imperial Presidency,* second edition (Boston: Houghton, Mifflin, 1989); Stephen Graubard, *Command of Office: How War, Secrecy, and Deception Transformed the Presidency from Theodore Roosevelt to George W. Bush* (New York: Basic Books, 2005); Robert H. Nelson, *Public Lands and Private Rights: The Failure of Scientific Management* (Lanham, MD: Rowan & Littlefield, 1995); Sally K. Fairfax, "When an Agency Outlasts its Time—A Reflection," *Journal of Forestry,* June-July, 2005,103(5): 264-267.
15. Gifford Pinchot, Forest Reserve Order No. 19, November 21, 1906, Forest History Society archives, with thanks to librarian Cheryl Oakes for its retrieval.
16. Mattison, "Devil's Tower National Monument," p. 6-7.
17. Rothman, *Preserving Different Pasts,* p. 74-76; 82-83.
18. Hal K. Rothman, *Navajo National Monument: A Place and Its People, an Administrative History* (Santa Fe, NM: Southwest Cultural Resources Center, Professional Papers No. 40, 1991), p. 13-49; see also, Peter Russell, *Gila Cliffs Dwelling National Monument: An Administrative History* (Santa Fe, NM: Southwest Cultural Resources Center, Professional Papers No. 46, 1992).
19. Rothman, *Preserving Different Pasts,* p. 89-91; 119-20.
20. Lee, "The Antiquities Act of 1906," *Journal of the Southwest,* p. 263-64; Gerald W. Williams, "National Monuments and the Forest Service," unpublished manuscript, November 13, 2003, p. 8-12; Alfred Runte, *National Parks: The American*

Experience, second edition (Lincoln: University of Nebraska Press, 1987); Rothman, *Preserving Different Pasts*, p. 187-209; Barry Mackintosh, *The National Parks: Shaping the System* (Washington, D.C.: NPS, 1991), p. 24–41.

21. Theodore Roosevelt, Speech at Grand Canyon, *The Coconino (Flagstaff) Sun*, May 9, 1903, p. 1, posted on http:www.kaibab.org/gc/gcps/teddy.htm and last accessed on March 12, 2005.

Rewilding the East
THE WEEKS ACT
AND THE EXPANSION OF FEDERAL FORESTRY

The Weeks Act, signed into law by President William Howard Taft on March 1, 1911, has had a profound impact on the American landscape, not least in New England. Just how profound is clear in a slick, two-page advertisement that the New Hampshire Division of Travel and Tourism Development ran in *Audubon Magazine* (May/June 2010). Wrapped around a series of photographs that capture the state's mountain vistas, rushing waters, tranquil lakes, and evocative sunsets, is a text that positively gushes: "Whether you're taking a wildlife tour, trekking along a mountain path, camping under the stars or simply drinking in the scenery, New Hampshire is full of unique places where you can interact with nature." One of the most spectacular is the White Mountain National Forest, which "features nearly 800,000 acres of unspoiled wilderness." New Hampshire is pristine.

A century ago, no one would have uttered these words about the Granite State; none would have dared called any part of it "unspoiled," at least not without considerable irony. By the late nineteenth century, the state had been cut over, farmed out, and burned up, thoroughly exploited, and utterly exhausted. This devastation, and the growing public outcry it produced, was one of the main reasons why the Weeks Act, which gave the federal government permission to purchase eastern forested lands for conservation purposes, was enacted.

Congress did not move to protect these battered landscapes without sustained grassroots pressure, however, and one of the key figures in this fight was a relatively obscure New Hampshire minister, the Reverend John E. Johnson. Licensed by the Episcopal Bishop of New Hampshire, for years Johnson had ministered to hardscrabble families throughout the rugged White Mountains region, and had come to know their struggles intimately. Whatever their personal foibles, Johnson asserted that the central source of their poverty and despair was the New Hampshire Land Company, "a corporation chartered to depopulate and deforest" a wide swath of the mountainous terrain. It was, Johnson thundered in a 1900 pamphlet, the "Worst 'Trust' in the World."

What made the company so egregious was the sweetheart deal it had negotiated with the state legislature that allowed its investors "to acquire for a song all the public lands thereabouts, and later 'take over' all tax titles, until finally there was no considerable tract in the vicinity which it did not own." Once it became the North Country's dominant landowner, the company began a process Johnson dubbed "refrigeration," in which it froze out local loggers by refusing to sell them the timber they needed to keep their small milling operations running. As a result, the next generation, "robbed of their winter employment, took no longer to the woods but to the cities, leaving the old folks to fall slowly but surely into the clutches of the company which took their farms from them or their heirs, in most cases for a dollar or two an acre." The cause of this tragic depopulation and desolation, Johnson asserted, "was due to the tightening of the coils of a boa constrictor *legalized* to crush the human life out of these regions preparatory to the stripping of them of their forests."[1]

Johnson's analysis was withering, if mono-causal: "it is amazing that the process of denuding this upper region of its forests in the most wasteful manner has not been arrested or at least hindered, long ago, and it probably would have been but for the fact that the whole business is largely in the hands of an unscrupulous and merciless corporation—a Trust of the most concentrated, ruthless and soulless character, which is bent on reducing entire sections to a blackened, hideous, howling wilderness."[2]

Yet his resolution was more complex, for he understood that zealous rhetoric alone would not stop the land company's depredations. Local pressure, statewide activism, regional support, and federal oversight were essential to the successful creation of a reform crusade that would insure social justice in and environmental protection for the White Mountains. In this fight, the minister asserted, the first and most important weapon was politics: "In the evolution of righteousness political economy precedes piety. The Law goes before the Gospel."[3]

The first step was to generate a public outcry—hence Johnson's pamphlet, which was designed to pressure the legislature to repair the physical and social landscape. The next was to establish an organization devoted to the restoration of the White Mountains and the local economy: Johnson was among those pushing for the creation of what would become the Society for the Protection of New Hampshire Forests; the SPNHF was launched in 1901, and its first president was the state's then-outgoing governor, Frank Rollins. "The last move will doubtless be to get a bill through the state legislature to purchase these deforested areas for a public reservation at a price ten times as great as that originally paid for the lumber lots," a skeptical Johnson predicted. His prediction dovetailed with *New England Homestead*'s calculation: "The lumber interests think they control the legislature," and so have hatched a scheme "to get off the lumber and wood, and in doing so create such a hue and cry that the public will be eager to pay a fancy price for the denuded lands." The progressive reformers knew they were complicit in this bit of greenmail, but believed that the end justified the means; to restore the land and the communities it once supported was worth what they anticipated would be a hefty price tag.[4]

New Hampshire, in the end, did not pick up the tab. The federal government did, through the aegis of the Weeks Act, enacted eleven years after Johnson's attack against the New Hampshire Land Company. Although the language of the national legislation contained none of Johnson's pulpit-thumping rhetoric or his energetic commitment to social betterment, it remains one of the most significant pieces of environmental legislation in U. S. political history.

Since 1911, for example, it has enabled the purchase of more than twenty million acres of private land located mostly in the eastern United States (although it also authorized funding to secure acreage in several western national forests). Some of the earliest purchases occurred in New Hampshire's White Mountains, a direct consequence of the SPNHF's active lobbying. The resulting White Mountain National Forest, formally created in May 1918, was not the first Weeks Act forest—that honor goes to North Carolina's Pisgah National Forest, established in 1916. But the question of which forest could claim seniority was of little interest to those who had advocated for the Weeks Act. The real point, they knew, was to build off these success stories in the northern and southern Appalachians. In the next decade, federal dollars led to the purchase of lands forming the Nantahala, Cherokee, George Washington, and Monongahela national forests. Then, with the 1924 passage of the Clarke-McNary Act (43 Stat. 653), the type of land the federal government could purchase was subtly expanded. Whereas the Weeks Act had limited purchases to the headwaters of navigable rivers such as the Merrimack, Monongahela, and Chattahoochee, Section 6 of the Clarke-McNary eased that hydrological restriction; now the Forest Service could negotiate to buy any "forested, cut-over, or denuded land within the watersheds of navigable streams as . . . may be necessary to the regulation of the flow of navigable streams or for the production of timber." Watersheds covered a lot of ground.

Just how much ground became clear during the Great Depression. Following Franklin Roosevelt's inauguration in 1933, a substantial amount of New Deal funding became available, in the end totaling more than $50 million. Additional sites came on line across the south, and a host of other forests and grasslands across the mid-west and central-plains states. The speed with which this process unfolded, and the significance that it held for the land recovery itself, is perhaps best captured in the experience in Mississippi. Between September 1933 and June 1934, a mere nine months, land surveys were conducted on and appraisals were approved for more than 600,000 acres.[5]

Mississippi may have been unique in this regard, but collectively the New Deal-era purchases represented a substantial increase of the nation's public-lands inventory. They also expanded the ability of the U. S. Forest Service to protect watersheds, regenerate heavily logged forests, replant overgrazed prairie, restore badly eroded and once-wooded lands, and develop innumerable recreational opportunities. Through the Weeks Act (and its subsequent amendments), the agency was able to operate in the East as it had done in the West. Put another way, this seminal legislation made the national forest system *national*; through it, conservation had gone continental.

Because the Weeks Act also sanctioned cooperation between Washington and the states in the shared pursuit of environmental regulation, it rearranged political relationships within the union; strengthened intergovernmental relations; and established more uniform land-management strategies. These developments were not entirely positive. In the aftermath of World War II, for example, the Forest Service's conviction that all fires must be suppressed at all times was reinforced by its adaptation of military surplus—bulldozers, communications technology, and aircraft—and a command-and-control mentality. These newfound capabilities were facilitated by the Weeks Act's initial creation of a robust fire-fighting regime in which state interests were subordinated to the federal agency's policy (a process that the Clarke-McNary Act later extended). It "made possible the extension of national standards of fire protection," historian Stephen Pyne has argued, making suppression "more uniform and more widely applicable." Depending on a forest's composition, this standardization could (and occasionally did) have disastrous results, leading to intense public debate over the value of excluding fire from diverse forested ecosystems around the country.[6]

Controversy swirled around another ramification of the Weeks Act's nationalization of forest policy, also most evident in the postwar era. Beginning in the 1950s, the Forest Service promoted a massive "Get Out the Cut" campaign; because privately owned timber supplies had shrunk due to intense logging for the war effort, the Forest Service accelerated harvests throughout the national forest system. As its clearcutting practices intensified, public protests erupted. Turkey hunters on the Monongahela National Forest blew the whistle on the agency's actions, and in *West Virginia Div. of Izaak Walton League of America, Inc. v. Butz* (1975) they and their allies successfully challenged the practice. That same year, *Zieske v. Butz* was decided: it stopped a planned 400,000-acre clear-cut for the Tongass National Forest in southeastern Alaska. And in Montana, residents in and around the Bitterroot National Forest went toe-to-toe with the agency over its "Oh My God" clearcuts (so called because your jaw dropped when you saw their massive size). Out of these legal battles and deepening debates emerged a new formulation of the Forest Service's mission, embodied in the 1976 National Forest Management Act (90 Stat. 2949), which effectively ended the practice of large-scale clearcutting.

A decade later, the issue simmered still. In New Hampshire no less a figure than former governor Sherman Adams took the agency to task, and did so with exquisite timing. In 1986, during the seventy-fifth anniversary celebrations of the Weeks Act that the Newcomen Society hosted, and at which Forest Service Chief Dale Robertson had introduced him, Adams challenged the agency's uncritical embrace of clearcutting: "After decades of using locally modified selective and selection cutting programs, the Forest Service had by 1962 incorporated in a wholesale, indiscriminate manner this aesthetically disruptive and, in forest conditions such as those prevalent in the White Mountains, scientifically questionable system." This "ill-advised national edict," he said, was a "disturbing threat to our New England tradition of consensus building among users of the White Mountains." As a consequence, "public confidence in the Forest Service was seriously shaken." It would take years before those frayed relations could be repaired.[7]

Yet the land's regeneration continued despite the explosive arguments over its condition and management. Surely one mark of its successful revival is the very unreflective quality of that 2010 advertisement urging tourists to visit leafy New Hampshire. By coming to this verdant and scenic state, it promised, they could "embrace the natural wonder of our land."[8]

That alluring claim would not have been possible without the Weeks Act, whose implementation over the succeeding century made New Hampshire—and a large number of other eastern, southern, and midwestern states—ever-more wild by law.

Notes

1. Rev. John E. Johnson, "The Boa Constrictor of the White Mountains, Or the Worst 'Trust' in the World" (pamphlet), July 4, 1900; reprinted in *New England Homestead*, December 8, 1900, 3-5.
2. *Ibid.*
3. *Ibid.*, 6; 11.
4. *Ibid.*, 4; *New England Homestead*, November 24, 1900, 508.
5. Ray M. Conarro, "The Beginning: Reflections and Comments" (Atlanta, GA: USDA-Forest Service, 1989), 1-2.
6. Stephen Pyne, *Fire in America: A Cultural History of Wildland and Rural Fire* (Princeton: Princeton University Press, 1982), 349-50.
. Sherman Adams, "The Weeks Act: A 75th Anniversary Appraisal," Newcomen Publication Number 1274 (New York: The Newcomen Society of the United States, 1987), 16-19.
8. *Audubon Magazine* (May/June 2010), 57.

Riding Herd on the Public Range

You have probably never heard of Pierre Grimaud. But whenever you pay to use one of the recreational-fee areas on the San Bernardino, Gifford Pinchot, or White Mountain national forests, you might want to thank him. The same is true the next time you get a permit to camp deep in the Bob Marshall or Gila wilderness areas. And if you have ever applied for a permit to run cattle or graze sheep within the folds of the Sierra, Wasatch, San Gabriel, or Rocky mountains, you now know to thank this same early twentieth-century shepherd.

Grimaud never knew that he would play a major role in helping to set the conditions by which twenty-first-century Americans could use the public lands. Certainly he had no idea that anyone would make a federal case out of his ill-advised decision in the early summer of 1907 to sneak his flock on to the Sierra Forest Reserve (now the Sierra National Forest). The first inkling of trouble he would have had was when a forest ranger stopped him and asked to see his permit. Grimaud admitted he did not have one, and with that he was on his way to court.

Yet so complex was this moment—raising as it did constitutional questions about Congress' ability to delegate administrative authority to other governmental entities (in this case the U. S. Forest Service)—that it took four years of legal wrangling before the dust had settled. Finally, on May 3, 1911, the U. S. Supreme Court determined that Grimaud was guilty as charged.

The Basque shepherd could not really play the innocent: he and his peers across California and the West had borne witness to the establishment of the first forest reserves, sanctioned under the 1891 Forest Reserve Act that empowered presidents to withdraw forests and grasslands from sale so as to protect these essential resources. Among the first western public lands that received this new designation were those in southern and central California: Presidents Harrison and Cleveland set aside units of what would become the Angeles (1892), Cleveland (1893), San Bernardino (1893) and Los Padres (1898) national forests; the Sierra was created in early 1893.

This initial federal presence expanded six years later when Congress enacted the so-called Organic Act of 1897, which granted management authority to the Department of the Interior, then the nation's sole custodian of the public domain. As part of this process, rangers were hired, and regulations were set for the use of these reserves' various resources, whether animal, vegetable, or mineral. And when in 1905 the U. S. Forest Service was established as part of the Department of Agriculture, and the nation's forests transferred to its care, the number of rangers increased again, the permitting process intensified, and the related rules and fees were published widely.

Just as broadly were they criticized, for few resource exploiters in the West found this new regime palatable. It was a rare newspaper that did not stoke the region's anger with scathing editorials and mocking cartoons. Miners, loggers, and ranchers challenged the agency's authority directly, through political agitation, and indirectly by furtively panning for gold and gems; cutting timber on the sly; and sneaking cattle, goats, and sheep on and off protected ranges.

California sheepherders like Grimaud were particularly adept at this deceptive practice: it was built into their annual cycle of grazing. In the winter months, their large flocks chewed up the Southern California rangelands in the coastal mountains and valleys. By spring, they had headed for greener pastures, roaming north through the Owens Valley, then at the height of summer scrambling up the Sierra's eastern face to graze its alpine meadows. As the days turned cooler, the herds began mowing down the western slope of the Sierra, the first leg of their journey south through the Central Valley and to their winter base. Along this lengthy migration—technically known as transhumance, the seasonal movement of people and their animals—there was little respect for or attention paid to the distinctions between public lands and private property, or the resultant grasslands devastation. As one contemporary critic in California wailed:

> There can be no doubt that sheepmen are a curse to the state; they
> penetrate everywhere, destroy the roots and seeds of the grasses;
> in traveling over the hills they keep the rocks and earth moving,
> destroying vegetation and denuding the hills of soil.[1]

Fed up, dust-choked communities along the trail petitioned the federal government for redress, and the speed with which the forest reserves were created to regenerate that battered terrain is itself a reflection of the pressing need to control the damage.

Grimaud's actions in running his sheep up into the Sierra Forest Reserve was thus part of a larger pattern of the use and abuse of the region's grasslands; his studied guile made it clear that he knew he was acting illegally, or so argued Justice Joseph Rucker Lamar, who delivered the Supreme Court's unanimous May 1911 opinion in *U. S v. Grimaud* (220 U. S. 506). Pierre Grimaud and his partner P. J. Carajous, the judge asserted:

> did knowingly, willfully, and unlawfully pasture and graze, and cause and procure to be pastured and grazed, certain sheep (the exact number being to the grand jurors unknown) upon certain land within the limits of and a part of said Sierra Forest Reserve, without having theretofore or at any time secured or obtained a permit or any permission for said pasturing or grazing of said sheep or any part of them, as required by the said rules and regulations of the Secretary of Agriculture.

This dense, cover-every-base language aside, the Supremes knew a con when they saw one.

Still, con law is a legal thicket, so Grimaud's case turned less on his uncontested willfulness than on his lawyers' creative defense of his actions. They rejected the charge that their client's behavior constituted a public offense against the United States because when Congress voted in support of the relevant forest legislation and accompanying ordinances, it was acting unconstitutionally; these "rules and regulations," they declared, were "an attempt by Congress to delegate its legislative power to an administrative officer." If, as they alleged, such delegation was unconstitutional, then Grimaud could not have committed a crime because there was no crime to commit.

Not buying that defensive maneuver was the grand jury that the U.S. District Court in the Southern District of California had empanelled to hear the case: in November 1907, its members upheld the prosecution's arguments, concluding that Pierre Grimaud had acted against the "peace and dignity of the United States." His attorneys immediately demurred, meaning the case would be heard before the District Court, a body that proved more susceptible to the defendant's pleadings. On a split vote, a majority agreed that Congress did not have the right or power to delegate its authority; Grimaud could not have committed a crime against regulations that did not have force.

This was one of many such cases that occurred throughout the region, and they were producing different results. Observed Phillip Wells, a lawyer working for the U. S. Forest Service: the "legal situation was very embarrassing to good administration because of conflicting decisions as to whether breach of Forest regulations could be punished by fine and imprisonment." Courts in Idaho, Arizona, and South Dakota, for instance, had sided with federal prosecutors. Those in southern California, Utah, and Washington had not. Particularly painful was the 1906 district court decision in the state of Washington. Reached "when the fight against the Service was hottest," Wells wrote, its rejection of federal grazing fees "was misrepresented by the hostile press throughout the West and by our enemies in Congress, notably by Senator Charles W. Fulton of Oregon, who, in an open letter, advised a constituent named Combs to graze his stock on the Forests in defiance of the regulations." It is little wonder that Grimaud's attorneys thought they had a very strong case.[2]

Federal prosecutors had a new trick up their sleeves, however. In 1907, the Criminal Appeals Act gave the government the right to appeal criminal cases, and in Wells' words "made it possible for the Service to get the question before the Supreme Court." They wasted little time. *U.S. v. Grimaud* was first argued in late February 1910 and reargued a year later. At long last, in May 1911, a unanimous court reversed the lower court's ruling, undercutting the defense by observing simply that the "authority to make administrative rules is not a delegation of legislative power." Grimaud's violation was punishable as a public offense.

This protracted argument may seem arcane but it is not. Had the Supreme Court sided with Grimaud; had it two days earlier sustained Fred Light, in *Light v. U.S.* (220 U. S. 523), a parallel case from Colorado, in which cattleman Light had been charged with letting his animals roam on a forest reserve without a permit, the one-two punch might well have knocked out the Forest Service. The fledgling agency would not have had the right to charge fees so as to control over-grazing on the grasslands under its care; its stewardship would have been handcuffed. That's the outcome many in the West desired, and why they were thrilled by the initial decision in *U. S. v. Grimaud*. That explains, too, why the Colorado state legislature went so far as to pay all of Fred Light's legal expenses. These opponents of federal-lands management hoped these two cases would set the stage for the implementation of a more-lax state control of the public domain.

The Supreme Court decisions dashed these hopes. Wrote an exultant Phillip Wells in 1913:

> The Light and Grimaud cases settled once and for all the
> constitutionality of the national conservation policy in so far as it
> is based upon and deals with the public lands and reservations of
> the United States. Over them, so *long as federal ownership continues,*

Congress has plenary power to sell, to reserve and lease, or to preserve without leasing, at its pleasure and can delegate to an administrative officer the duty of reserving or leasing and of defining and prohibiting trespass. The organized resistance of the stockmen collapsed and thereafter the protection of the forests from grazing trespass was a mere matter of routine police duty.[3]

A smart lawyer, Wells knew his italicized caveat lay at the heart of the matter. So have successive generations of western legislators and resource extractors who ever since have continued to dispute federal ownership of the public lands and its land-management regulations. A series of Sagebrush Rebellions have roiled regional politics since the twentieth century, and have included lawsuits frivolous and furious, hostile congressional hearings, vituperative talk-show condemnations, and, occasionally, violence. In the 1980s, the commissioners of Nye County, Nevada, rammed bulldozers into Forest Service gates, symbolically laying claim to federal property; in the same decade, vigilantes took pot-shots at agency offices and booby-trapped official vehicles. Thirty years later, in the immediate aftermath of Republican victories in the 2010 congressional elections, right-wing commentators and Tea Party politicians started trying to stir up yet another revolt in the run-up to the 2012 presidential election.[4]

Yet for all their energetic animus to federal law, to date none of these attempts have succeeded in dislodging the precedent-setting reality on the ground that a California shepherd unknowingly established when he drove his flock up into a high-country meadow. In doing so, Grimaud insured that the entire national forest system would long endure.

Notes

1. Anthony Godfrey, *The Ever-Changing View: A History of the National Forests in California* (Washington, D. C.: Government Printing Office, 2005), p. 59-60.
2. Phillip P. Wells to Gifford Pinchot, March 21, 1913, reprinted in "Phillip P. Wells in the Forest Service Law Office," *Forest History*, April 1972, 24.
3. *Ibid.*, 25.
4. "The Sagebrush Rebellion," *U.S. News & World Report*, December 1, 1980; http://www2.vcdh.virginia.edu/PVCC/mbase/docs/sagebrush.html; last accessed June 14, 2011.

Place Making

Devils Postpile National Monument, despite its wonderfully lurid name, is not much of a draw. Located near Mammoth Lakes in the eastern Sierra, it is small, a mere 798 acres. It can be buried under more than four hundred inches of snow a year, so its visiting season is a short four months. Even the pile to which its name refers—a columnar basalt structure, formed from a lava flow that may date back one hundred thousand years—is not particularly unusual; such structures can be found across the globe.

Curiously, it also wasn't the first national monument named after Beezlebub; that nod goes to Devils Tower, founded in 1906. Neither can it claim the same kind of legendary status attached to such sites as Arizona's Petrified Forest (1906), California's Muir Woods (1908), and Utah's Mukuntuweap, which later morphed in Zion National Park (1909). And compared to the Grand Canyon, originally protected via national-monument designation in 1906—well, nothing compares to the canyon.

However small and unnoticed it may be, Devils Postpile should draw the curious and mobile, for the site's geology, like its human history, testifies to why earlier conservationists fought so hard to protect it and other iconic landscapes-turned-monuments in the American west.

Not that Euro-America explorers or settlers in eastern California had much to say about the postpile. Even the loquacious John Muir, namesake of the famed hiking trail that runs through the landmark, said little about it prior to 1910 (more on that later). His silence is surprising: you couldn't get him to shut up about the geological wonders of the Yosemite or how glaciers had done so much to carve its magnificent contours.

Yet every bit as fascinating is the valley in which Devils Postpile is located, which millennia ago was filled with lava to a depth of four hundred feet; as the molten mass cooled, settled, and shrank it did so gradually enough that the postpile's columnar structure maintained its celebrated regularity. This physical characteristic could only become apparent after the massive ice flow that subsequently filled the basin retreated: its force had quarried much of the volcanic material, but it left exposed a largely intact fragment of the original structure. In the intervening years—ten thousand or so— segments of the column fell away, piling up at the base like so many logs; this led some nineteenth-century mapmakers to call it Devil's Woodpile. Had Muir clambered to its top, he would have seen, as he had with such great clarity in nearby Yosemite, the scouring power of ice, nature's buff and polish.

The human imprint is less immediately visible. But it's there. Start with the site's boundary lines, which have changed over time. The establishment of Yosemite National Park in 1890 included the postpile region, not because of its special value—few then knew of it—but as a result of aggressive surveying. Or re-surveying. This iteration of the park actually marked its re-establishment: in June 1864, as General U.S. Grant waged his brutal Wilderness Campaign in Virginia, President Abraham Lincoln signed Yosemite's initial enabling legislation, placing portions of the fabled terrain under state control. By the late 1880s, Muir, his ally *Century Magazine* editor Robert Underwood Johnson, and other conservationists started agitating for full national park status. In October 1890, they prevailed. Understandably, those responsible for mapping out this latest version of the park sought to incorporate as much territory as possible.

Their ambition set up the first controversy in which Devils Postpile figured, if indirectly. In 1905, as the Theodore Roosevelt administration negotiated with Congress over the creation of the U. S. Forest Service and a national-forest system, lobbyists for mining, grazing, and logging interests made a play to shrink Yosemite, stripping away acreage that then would be shifted to the new agency. They pushed for this transfer because the Forest Service's soon-to-be mission was to allow regulated resource extraction, making local mineral deposits, grasslands, and timber available for use. The Sierra Club, which over the years had fought off attacks on the park's extent, failed this time. Roosevelt signed off on the transfer of approximately five hundred square miles, much of which would become first part of the Sierra National Forest (and later the Inyo National Forest).

The import of this change of administrative venue became clear five years later. Water-resource proponents began scheming to dam the middle fork of the San Joaquin River, whose captured streamflow would power nearby mining operations. This action would have submerged the postpile, and, adding insult to injury, there was talk of first blasting the geological formation and using its "logs" as part of the new reservoir's bulwark.

The timing of this 1910 project could not have been coincidental. It was submitted during the intense national debate over the construction of what would become the O'Shaughnessy Dam in the Hetch Hetchy Valley, and its advocates may have expected that this tumultuous moment offered perfect cover for their proposal. If so, they did not count on Walter L. Huber, a Forest Service civil engineer, to whom they submitted their brief.

He was appalled. Arguing that the plan was "a wanton destruction of scenery" (long before the agency itself promoted scenic values), Huber urged his superiors to press President William Howard Taft to designate what was then called Devil's Postpile (note the possessive) as a national monument. John Muir and the Sierra Club proper, along with distinguished University of California scientists such as Joseph N. LeConte, joined the chorus, sending petitions to the White House and to the Secretaries of Agriculture and Interior. Suddenly, Devil's Postpile was on the map.

The resolution that the protesters pushed for would not have been possible five years earlier. But in 1906, Congress had passed the Antiquities Act (16 USC 431-433), which granted the chief executive extraordinary powers. Its key second section reads:

> That the President of the United States is hereby authorized, in his discretion, to declare by public proclamation historic landmarks, historic and prehistoric structures, and other objects of historic or scientific interest that are situated upon the lands owned or controlled by the Government of the United States to be national monuments, and may reserve as a part thereof parcels of land, the limits of which in all cases shall be confined to the smallest area compatible with proper care and management of the objects to be protected ...

I hope you caught the essential phrase: "in his discretion." These three words allow the president to create national monuments without consulting Congress. Starting with Teddy Roosevelt, who by the stroke of his pen created eighteen of them, many chief executives have followed suit.

Even George W. Bush. Although not the most environmentally minded of presidents, in 2006 he unilaterally established Papahānaumokuākea Marine National Monument (covering 140,000 square miles, extending northwest from Hawaii); and three years later inked the founding documents for the Pacific Remote Islands National Monument, sweeping across 86,000 square miles of the central Pacific.

Taft wasn't a staunch conservationist, either. In January 1910, he had enraged those who were when he fired Gifford Pinchot as the Forest Service chief for publicly challenging the administration's decision to relinquish prime coalfields in Alaska to a New York syndicate; and for alleging thereby that the president was dismantling Roosevelt's environmental commitments. The resulting furor consumed the rest of Taft's one-term presidency.

Amid the uproar—and perhaps to prop up his sagging reputation—on July 6, 1911, our twenty-seventh president put his signature on Proclamation 1166 (37 Stat. 1715):

> Whereas the natural formations known as the Devil Postpile and Rainbow Falls, within the Sierra National Forest, in the State of California, are of scientific interest, and it appears that the public interests will be promoted by reserving said formations as a National Monument; Now, therefore, I, William H. Taft, President of the United States ... do proclaim that there are hereby reserved from all forms of appropriation under the public. Land laws, subject to all prior valid adverse claims, and set apart as a National Monument, all the tracts of land in the State of California shown as the Devil Postpile National Monument. ..." By these words did he turn Devil Postpile (someone, somewhere dropped the possessive!) into the country's twenty-eighth monument.

Not a lot of people noticed, however it was spelled, whatever its place on the numerical listing of sites. Because the area was well off the beaten track, with only a poorly maintained mining road for access, the number of visitors was few. The Forest Service, which then had management responsibilities for the national monument (but no budget to do so), posted signs about its legal status and left it at that; other agencies did the same for their sites, a strategy of dubious value.

A more pronounced protection policy finally emerged during the Great Depression. Via an inside-the-cabinet coup, in 1934 Franklin Roosevelt's Interior Secretary Harold Ickes arranged to have all national monuments, including Devils Postpile, transferred to the National Park Service (NPS). This transfer strengthened the Park Service's mission, making it essentially the only federal agency charged with managing the nation's significant geologic, historic, or cultural resources.

In retrospect, this exclusivity seems like a mistake; as a consequence neither the Forest Service nor the Bureau of Land Management has had a major commitment to, because they have not had the mandated funding for, historic preservation or the promotion of history itself. But for NPS, Ickes' deft maneuver gave it an expanded workload and larger budget, enabling it for the first time to station a ranger at Devils Postpile during the summer months. This assignment continued until World War Two, when, because of funding losses, the Park and Forest services struck a deal in which the latter took responsibility for the monument; in 1952, NPS regained the supervisory role, and has maintained it ever since. But the two agencies have continued to collaborate, as the monument, completely surrounded by the Inyo National Forest, makes ready use of the Forest Service's heavy-duty snow-removal equipment; and for thirty years they have shared a shuttle service operated by the Eastern Sierra Transit Authority to bring visitors into and out of these public lands, minimizing the impact of automobiles on the air quality and aesthetic appeal of these Sierran high-country landscapes.

A different kind of cooperation is woven into the history of Devils Postpile, revealing as it does the complex manner by which Americans have negotiated (and renegotiated) their relationship with the natural world. It was not enough that this particular geological formation was unusual in North America. It had to be identified as important, which required scientific explanation and a cultural receptivity to the fact of its newly proclaimed "value." The postpile also required a committed group of people, experts and activists, to fight in its defense, once that they knew what to fight for; it needed as well a legislative initiative that could transform its legal status; and the near-simultaneous creation of a pair of new federal land-management agencies—the Forest Service (1905) and the Park Service (1916), each with different missions—that could be entrusted with its care through the work of a new occupation, the ranger. Not until adequate roads were constructed, however, could the all-important tourist come to see what the fuss was about, and once there become schooled about its import through a peculiar innovation, the ranger-led evening campfire.

At those summer gatherings, as sparks whirl up into the dark sky and the Milky Way wheels overhead, I hope the rangers thread together the two kinds of history that have converged at Devils Postpile: the geological record that captures the pressures that over tens of thousands of years formed, exposed, and then burnished the basalt column; and the much shorter period of time—a mere thirty years or so—that it took Americans to invent the language and social institutions required to protect this chunk of hardened minerals.

A malleable earth and a nimble human imagination were essential to the making of what we now call Devils Postpile National Monument.

Fire Fight

Mt. Gleason Fire Camp 16 sits atop a rocky ridge separating the North Fork of Mill Creek and the Gleason Canyon drainages, situated deep inside the Angeles National Forest. It is brutally rough country, with steep slopes falling away at 70° angles, and quite inaccessible. To reach the camp, you have to drive six miles out along a winding, narrow road off the Angeles Forest Highway. Its very remoteness made it a perfect site for a Nike Missile base, which the U. S. Army maintained there between 1956 and 1974. Its isolation also helped determine its subsequent use: in 1979, Camp 16 was constructed under a cooperative arrangement between the Los Angeles County Fire Department and the California Department of Corrections and Rehabilitation, and has served as a fire-fighting training facility that can house more than one hundred inmates.

None of those stationed there on August 26, 2009, could have known that within days their training would be severely tested. But that afternoon, an arsonist ignited a small patch of vegetation not far from the Angeles Crest Ranger Station. The first report came in at 3:20 p.m., and within eleven minutes Forest Service personnel noted that the fire already had ballooned to "three acres and running." It did not stop until what came to be called the Station Fire had blackened more than 160,000 acres, a holocaust whose convective energy created its own micro-climates, including pyro-cumulus clouds that billowed thousands of feet into the sky; its smoke darkened such distant cities as Las Vegas and Denver.

From afar, that churning column of smoke, gas, and heat signaled the fire's ferocity. So it was for those on the ground and in the air who battled to control the swirling flames. But these firefighters also came to understand that this ominous formation intensified the event's unpredictability: as it periodically blew up and collapsed, the whole acted like a bellows, sucking up and then flinging fiery brands a mile in advance of the main blaze; its powerful downdrafts and erratic winds then fanned the embers. It didn't help that the pine trees and live oaks, chaparral, manzanita, and other vegetation that clothed the canyons, ridgelines, and mountain faces were tinder dry; or that the atmosphere was superheated; or that humidity was almost nonexistent. Adding to the danger was that portions of this landscape, especially around Camp 16, had not burned since the 1919 San Gabriel Canyon and Ravenna fires. Fuel loads—of woody material live and dead—were of far greater volume than they otherwise might have been, an estimated forty tons per acre.

None of this boded well for the veteran firefighters assigned to defend the camp or for the inmate-trainees who lived there. Although they all knew on the morning of August 30 that the fire was running in their direction, and as a precaution had combed the site's perimeter and grounds, clearing away flammable debris; and although they rehearsed exactly what steps they must take to protect themselves, the fire's ground speed and ferocious energy took them by surprise. "The entire bowl of heavy fuels below the camp exploded over the camp," the official incident report declared, "igniting a crown fire that pulled the fire through the camp and into the tree plantation north of Camp 16."

Hoping to slow, perhaps even deflect, the scorching rush, at 4:20 p.m. the superintendent of Camp 16, Captain Ted Hall, and Arnie Quinones, foreman of Crew 16-3, drove to an access road beneath the camp to begin backfiring operations, using a drip torch and a Very pistol. In the face of searing, howling winds, their efforts were to no avail. As conditions rapidly deteriorated around them, the two men returned to their truck and tried to race through the hissing flames, thick smoke, and blistering heat to safety, only veer over a berm and plunge into the roaring canyon.

Their deaths are a stark reminder of the human costs associated with firefighting in the Angeles National Forest. Alas, Hall and Quinones join a long list of those who over the past century have given their lives in defense of Southern California's communities and landscapes. Since its establishment in May 1911, the LA County Fire Department alone has lost an estimated seventy-six firefighters, a mark of the dangers inherent in this profession, and of these individuals' sense of dedication and duty.

Personality and training notwithstanding, these generations of firefighters have also put themselves on the line in part because of Stuart J. Flintham. He is credited with developing the LA County department's fire-fighting mission and launching many of the infrastructural initiatives that since have become essential to the attempt to suppress the region's often-furious wildland fires. Yet when he was hired in January 1912 as the county forester, there was no department to speak of. Flintham was the third to have held the position in seven months. In accordance with the state's 1909 Shade Tree Act, the Los Angeles County Board of Forestry was created with the initial focus on the planting and maintenance of roadside trees. The appointed body hired its first forester on October 1, but he resigned before the month was out, and was replaced by an interim appointee who served until Flintham secured the position.

Born in New York in 1879, Flintham was well educated—he did his undergraduate work at Williams College and finished his bachelor's in forestry at Cornell University. He was well trained, too—in 1904, he received his M.A. from the Yale School of Forestry, then in its fourth year of operation; Gifford Pinchot and his family had endowed the nation's first graduate program in the science of land management, and the legendary conservationist had helped devise its curriculum. Naturally enough, after graduation Flintham's first job was with Pinchot's Forest Service, serving as a forest inspector in California. In 1907, he was appointed supervisor of the Stanislaus National Forest, yet within a year Pinchot had fired Flintham; the chief was "displeased with the way [Flintham] interacted with people."

This negative description of Flintham would have surprised those who three years later began working with him as he industriously set up the LA county forester's office. They found him an engaging presence who tackled his array of duties with dispatch. Flintham and his small staff managed and extended roadside tree-plantings along many of the boulevards and arterial streets across the county. He also initiated reforestation and afforestation projects in the foothills and high-country watersheds.

Most consuming was the effort required to build a network of fire companies throughout the then-extensive unincorporated areas, linking them together in terms of equipment purchased and deployed and the uniformity and consistency of employee training. Having been the driving agent behind the formation of forty fire districts, for which he served as their collective chief, Flintham succeeded in assembling what a contemporary characterized as the "State's largest fire-fighting organization outside of a municipality." His ambition for Los Angeles was much like that of his Forest Service peers for the larger American west—stamp out fire.

To accomplish this required a pragmatism and flexibility that as a young national-forest superintendent Flintham may not have enjoyed. But these qualities appear to have been on full display in his work in greater Los Angeles. "Mr. Flintham was one of the best known men of the county, from the desert, over the mountains [and] to the sea," asserted a colleague. "Hardly a town or community but what at some time or other had called him in for advice on fire protection or planting of trees and shrubs."

Flintham's greatest impact, however, may have been in his pioneering management of Southern California's wildland fires. Drawing on his forestry training at Yale, and subsequent fieldwork for the Forest Service; and making immediate use of some of the lessons that he and his professional colleagues learned in the wake of the devastating Big Burn of 1910, which torched nearly three million acres in Washington, Idaho, and Montana, Flintham devised a systemic approach to identifying, monitoring, and, where possible, suppressing firestorms.

This included securing labor and budgets to cut hundreds of miles of firebreaks that snaked up foothills and ridgelines; using horses, mules, and vehicles to mount patrols during fire season; and constructing lookout towers to increase surveillance capabilities. First utilizing the telephone to speed up communication between firefighters on the ground, by the early 1920s the county force was making clever use of a home-built mobile radio unit to coordinate its efforts. Even the local U. S. Army air squadron was enlisted: its bi-planes provided aerial-mapping services and conducted fire overflights. In 1924, Flintham's deft administration earned the praise of one of his Yale classmates, William B. Greeley, then chief of the Forest Service. After inspecting the LA County forestry program, he reported to *American City Magazine* that it was "exceptionally well organized and eminently progressive."

Months later, the San Gabriel fire, which erupted on August 31 and over the next twenty-seven days burned upwards of fifty thousand acres, tested this organizational structure and the pre-existing cooperative arrangements between LA County and the federal agency. Like the Station Fire, this blaze was big, fast, and furious. Watching its five-mile-wide front advance led a witness to write that the whole mountain range was on fire, "with hissing flames leaping skywards as thrown with fury from the bowels of the earth." Its ferocity, like that of the early-twenty-first-century blaze, drew on all available resources, human and technological, and frustrated those who tried desperately to put it down. One source of that frustration—suggested in the fire's sudden and swift surges up and down the jagged canyons— may have been meteorological: a photograph from Mt. Wilson captures a towering smoke plume that might have propelled these flames as did the pyro-cumulus cloud that energized the massive 2009 conflagration.

Although the Forest Service was in charge of the 1924 firefight in the Angeles National Forest, Flintham quickly offered his office's aid. This was routine. As he had noted two years earlier in his department's annual report: "Since a large portion of our mountain water-sheds lie within the Angeles and Santa Barbara [now Los Padres] National Forests, the department has joined with the Forest Service administration on every large fire." But this time he was rebuffed. Forest Supervisor Rushton Charlton—another Cornell forestry alum—assumed his crews could handle the human-ignited fire and did not accept help for several days. In the end, the LA County firefighters were more fully integrated in the month-long struggle, a force that swelled to two thousand. One of them was Flintham. Lauded as "the type of man who fought his fires right on the line rather than from a swivel chair," he put in "such long hours and heavy work ... that on the last day when the fire was brought under control he collapsed on Mt. Wilson." His coworkers believed that this extended period of stress, combined with a set of already diagnosed ulcers, led to the forty-six-year-old forester's untimely demise in June 1925.

Flintham's formative and formidable commitment to attacking fire in the Southland's rugged mountains, among the most challenging terrain in the country, has done much to protect the sprawling community's built environment. It has also exacted a high cost, as attested to by the number of names emblazoned on LA County's memorial wall to fallen firefighters. Yet that monument, amazingly enough, contains only two such names from the inferno that in 2009 consumed Camp 16. Despite two-hundred-foot-long flames flashing over the site, ember showers of immense intensity, and the incineration of every building in the compound, seventy-two personnel safely retreated to an already burned space to their immediate north, sheltering in place for the next ninety minutes or so as the firestorm torched everything in its path.

In their fortunate survival lies a message that the official incident report underscores: defending structures during conflagrations of the size of the Station Fire is tricky at best; it becomes even more so under the extreme heat and unstable weather conditions that prevailed on August 30, 2009, dangers that the site's difficult topography and dense fuel load amplified. Rethinking the felt need to protect that which is expendable—a pulling back that such federal agencies as the Forest Service, National Park Service, and Bureau of Land Management have undertaken since the 1990s—is the most enduring way to memorialize the special bravery of Ted Hall and Arnie Quinones.

Reefer Madness

Summer 2010 was a busy time on the Angeles National Forest. The Forest Service and its contractors poured lots of time and energy into restoring the badly burned terrain in the aftermath of the 2009 Station fire. CalTrans and its crews labored to reconstruct the torched, eroded, and washed-out roads that had been damaged during the historic blaze that consumed 250 square miles. Although shut out from the scorched portions of the San Gabriel Mountains, tens of thousands of Angelenos recreated along its trails, creeks, and rivers—hiking, running, biking, and fishing. They gamboled in this island of green set within a sea of concrete.

Some of that green was a bit more worrisome than others: across that summer and early fall, Forest Service officers collaborated with LA County sheriffs and other law-enforcement agencies in raiding marijuana-growing sites on the Angeles that were scattered across some of its most remote and difficult landscapes.

By that late June, they already had destroyed upwards of ninety-six thousand plants, a cash crop worth an estimated $192 million. Then, in early July, members of the U.S. Drug Enforcement Agency teamed up with local forces on two major busts in the vicinity of Fish Canyon and Knapp Ranch. With police helicopters whirling overhead, the eradication teams weeded out more than eleven thousand plants valued at $22 million; as with other such efforts, they also cleaned out almost a ton of trash, irrigation pipes, herbicides and chemical fertilizers, tools and other material the growers had used to manage their illegal crop.

Later that month, the task force once again hit paydirt: after getting reports from hikers of suspicious activities in the forest, it sent three teams up a series of ridgelines and creekbeds, discovering forty-one sites that were home to nearly seventeen thousand plants (street value: $35 million). Streams had been diverted by crude check dams whose flow then was piped to the cultivated fields; crews spent days cleaning out the irrigation systems and sweeping up the hazardous waste, and nearly a thousand pounds of garbage were airlifted out of the narrow canyons.

Even less accessible was a four-acre plot located in late September, half a mile up a steep, chaparral-choked slope in Cow Canyon, off the Glendora Ridge Road near Mt. Baldy Village. To get to it, agents had to bushwhack into this rough country; they just missed capturing their grower—a radio was blaring when the team arrived at the site. As some officers eradicated six hundred and fifty plants, others stripped out irrigation infrastructure, bagged trash, and returned the nearby creek to its natural course, clearing the way for restoration crews to revegetate the cutover slope.

These are only some of the reported incidents during the summer of 2010, a reflection of the serious impact marijuana production is having on the Angeles National Forest, and on the three other national forests draped across the coastal ranges of Southern California; warm-weather raids took place as well on the San Bernardino, Cleveland, and Los Padres forests. "These illegal marijuana grows do more than just harm the people who use illicit marijuana, they destroy and poison public lands," affirmed Captain Ralph Ornelas of the LA County Sheriff's Narcotics Bureau. "The many agencies involved in these operations will continue our aggressive efforts to clear the public land of this menace, so that the forest remains available for present and future generations."

That's pretty tough talk. It seems justified, too, for the Angeles National Forest has become a key node in the regional production and distribution of marijuana, which Los Angeles County Sheriff Lee Baca has argued has become a $1.2 billion industry. Yet however substantial its economic impact in Southern California may be, it is nothing compared to the massive output that flows out of the so-called Emerald Triangle in northern California: Humboldt, Lake, and Mendocino counties—and particularly the national and state forests that lie within this fertile region—are responsible for approximately 80 percent of the state's illegal growing. That's a ton of weed.

Actually, it may run as high as 49,105 metric tons. So reports the U.S. Office of National Drug Control Policy, which issued data on the last four years of eradication efforts in California. With 2006 as its baseline, when 2,642,352 plants were seized, the number climbed to 4,961,313 in 2007; rose to 5,432,053 in 2008, and one year later soared to 7,519,580 plants. The report assumes that this impressive spike (over a 300 percent increase in that time) is a reflection of an intensification of production across those years; and it also assumes that the authorities may be interdicting but 15 percent of that which is being grown outdoors. The agency's conservative estimate of what authorities did not capture is forty-nine million plants.

This data reveals the enormity of the policing problem facing National Forest rangers, county sheriffs, and federal law-enforcement officers. It also suggests some of the profound consequences for the land itself. After all, to prepare even a small site requires hacking down trees and clearing away undergrowth, which can lead to significant erosion. To nourish the marijuana plants and suppress weeds growers spray gallons of chemical fertilizers and herbicides, toxic material that can leach into ground and surface waters. The same goes for the improper disposal of human waste. Garbage piles attract rats and other invasive species. Blocking streams compromises riparian habitat and harms the wildlife that depends on it.

Wildlife suffers in other ways. There is "no grey area when it comes to this aspect of illegal marijuana grows," restoration experts have confirmed; "the wildlife is killed, plain and simple. Traps are set, deer, bear, and grey squirrels are poached, and mice are poisoned. Based on the tools that have been collected and the carcasses that have been identified, the growers are engaged in a war with the natural world for the resources they require to continue their production of marijuana."

The concentrated effort to stop this despoliation is frustrating and incessant, which is why the local, state, and federal agents engaged in this oft-dangerous work often refer to themselves as the Thin Green Line. They do not see their actions simply as a piece of the controversial War on Drugs, but as a battle to protect and preserve imperiled landscapes. Yet there is not enough money or labor to do this critical rehab work. In 2010, for instance, volunteer restoration teams managed to reclaim seventy sites across the state, but more than eight hundred had been identified. Still, they and law enforcement do what they can.

Or do what they feel they must. Lt. John Nores, Jr., of California's Department of Fish and Game, makes this case in *War in the Woods: Combating the Marijuana Cartels on America's Public Lands*, a hyped-up if compelling account of the anguish he and his comrades feel at the end of each operation. Notwithstanding the book's evocation of Vietnam— camouflaged strike forces slipping though a dense tangle wary of booby traps and well-armed growers—it also advocates full restoration of the abused land. Just before taking down an illegal dam that fed a major cultivation site along Bonjetti Creek in the eastern face of the Santa Cruz Mountains, Nores muses:

> The creek water above the dam is clean, clear, and cold, just like a high-mountain trout stream in California's Sierra Nevada. The surrounding ferns, grasses, and thick tree canopies above the creek are similarly pristine and beautiful. ... Standing here I have a hard time imagining that more than a million people are hustling around the San José area only a short distance from us, and yet these amazing natural areas

are so close and provide so much to our environment and its wildlife species.

For him, this particular incident was not just another drug bust.

Stopping such "environmental crimes" will increase in complexity in the coming years. Drug cartels have figured out that growing marijuana on U. S. national forests is a good deal cheaper and easier than trying to smuggle it across the now-thoroughly militarized US-Mexico border. The same calculation is at work in the eastern national forests, where meth labs are proliferating. That in Southern California there are four national forests and lots of state and local public lands close to the region's massive population and its robust network of freeways only adds to their focus on this regional market and its massive transportation grid.

Surely those factors help account for this ominous statistic: in 2009, Los Angeles County recorded the fifth-highest number of plant seizures in California. It wasn't in the top ten in 2006.

Landscape Mosaic
MANAGING FRAGMENTED FORESTS

The important ecological interconnections between public and private lands are widely recognized, most recently in the form of ecosystem management. But what is the historical and political relationship between national-forest management and private-land development? And how might the U.S. Forest Service respond to increased private-land development and landscape fragmentation? There are historical lessons that might guide policy makers and national-forest managers even as they confront the unprecedented challenges posed by an increase in land fragmentation, which range from the construction of housing subdivisions in the wildland urban interface (WUI) to corporate timberland divestment.

Early in the 2000s, the Forest Service began to recognize the problem that development posed for the public lands under its care, and to formulate a policy response to it. The agency, for example, has targeted the loss of open space as one of the "four threats" to the health of the nation's forests and grasslands, and the Resources Planning Act (RPA) Assessment provides the empirical basis for such concern. In 2006, then-Chief Dale Bosworth argued that "National Forests are becoming islands in a sea of urban, suburban, and exurban development," noting that because of obvious public-private spillovers "focusing on our own turf just isn't feasible anymore."[1]

In devising a strategy for conserving open space, the agency has solicited input and ideas from various stakeholders, but because this essay examines the subject from a historical and policy perspective, it is positioned to bring to the discussion a few ideas and questions that require greater attention than they have received. This is especially important because national-forest management will become even more contested in the future, due to intensifying development on private lands, and there are a number of policy and planning tools that can be used to deal with the resultant debates and disputes.

Let's start with the uncontested: population growth, private-land development, and the divestment of corporate timberlands to real-estate schemes and subdivision developments pose a unique challenge to natural-resource management on America's public lands. To understand just how big a challenge, consider the following statistics:

• The U.S. population is expected to increase by more than 120 million people over the next fifty years[2]
• Between 1982 and 2001, 34 million acres of open space (roughly the size of Illinois) were developed, approximately 4 acres per minute or 6,000 acres per day[3]
• From 1990 to 2000, 60 percent of all new housing units in the U.S. were built in the WUI, and by 2000, about 38 percent of housing units overall were located in the WUI[4]
• Between 1982 and 1997, over 10 million acres of forests were converted to houses, buildings, lawns, and pavement, with another 26 million acres projected to be developed by 2030. All together, the total loss of forests will be close to the size of Georgia[5]
• Total forest area is projected to decrease by roughly 23 million acres by 2050[6]
• Forty-four million acres of private forests could see sizable increases in housing density by 2030[7]
• Between 1983 and 2009, 37.7 million acres of industrial timberland in the U.S. was transferred out of industry ownership[8]
• From 1982 to 1997, 3.2 million acres of rangeland were converted to developed land. And another 25 million acres of "strategic ranch lands" arc estimated to be at risk of residential development by 2020[9]

The Forest Service has thoroughly documented the interrelationship between these social pressures and private-lands development, as have the USDA research stations and scholars publishing in such venues as the *Journal of Forestry*. The trends and implications have been analyzed from numerous angles, such as the ecological effects of parcelization, biodiversity, fire management, urban forestry, among others. Largely missing from these appraisals, however, is a historical assessment and overtly political analysis of these patterns, real and projected. This essay begins filling the void in the literature by laying out some ideas and questions that need to be considered in formulating policies responding to the problems that private-land development poses for the national forests.[10]

By precept and policy, the Forest Service has always been in dialogue with those landowners whose properties abut the national forests. This interaction between those who manage public lands and private landowners has deep roots. They stretch back to the establishment of the USDA Division of Forestry (1881), which, under the direction of Franklin B. Hough, tracked the rapid harvesting of U. S. woodlands; these data led

Hough to urge that the "principal bodies of timber land still remaining the property of the government ... be withdrawn from sale." This was arguably the first time that an official had linked the need for protection to the scale and speed of harvests on private and (some) federal lands, but it would not be the last. One of his successors, Bernhard Fernow, the division's third director, also advocated for greater governmental protection as a result of escalating cutting and suggested that holding federal-lands timber off the market might stabilize then-falling prices.[11]

But neither Hough nor Fernow had the legal authority to put their ideas into action. That constraint began to change with the enactment of the Forest Reserve Act (1891), which gave presidents the power to create federal forest reserves; and the Organic Act (1897), which allowed for the management of the reserves. In 1898, Fernow retired and Gifford Pinchot became the new head of the forestry division; the young American forester hoped to take advantage of the changing legal environment to provide greater control over these federal lands and the resources—timber, mineral, and grass—that they contained.

There was a complication, however. The federal forests were under the Department of Interior's control, while Pinchot and the Division of Forestry were housed in Agriculture, complicating the young forester's ambition to introduce forest management to the public lands. He finessed this problem in two ways, contracting with Interior to help regulate its timber sales and launching an innovative public-private initiative announced in *Circular 21* (1898). With the latter's publication, the forestry division offered to "help farmers, lumbermen, and other private timberland owners apply Forestry to their holdings." According to Pinchot, "[t]his was our major offensive," providing "working plans for conservative lumbering, with full directions for practical work, and assistance on the ground." Out of this partnership, he believed, would grow and flow a much-needed mutual respect: federal foresters would learn more about private timber owners' dilemmas and gain greater public support for practical forestry. Another result of Circular 21's implementation may have been some timber-price stabilization, linked to the reduction in the number of small operators with access to forest-reserve timber. Even though Circular 21's *raison d'etre* disappeared in 1905 when the nation's forests were transferred from Interior to Agriculture, three years later Pinchot created the Division of State and Private Forestry inside the Forest Service to continue its cooperative, public-private policies.[12]

A collaborative emphasis also emerged in response to another peculiar historical circumstance: many public-domain acres that eventually became part of the national-forest inventory existed side-by-side with the so-called "checkerboard" lands. These fragments were a legacy of nineteenth-century federal land surveys, which carved out 640-acre lots, and railroad land grants, which gave corporations alternating mile-square sections they could sell to pay for railway construction. Because those segments located in mountainous terrain were difficult to offload, they often remained in private hands; the presence of these and other intermingled lands ever since have compelled the agency to coordinate its management with these other owners.

In the early years, this coordination, framed by economic realities, limited harvests on the national forests. In 1912, Forester R. M. Evans observed that, owing "to the inaccessibility of the Government timber and to the large amount of privately owned timber surrounding it, there is no immediate prospect of a large sale." After World War Two, the same thing occurred but this time the reduction was "at the specific request of industry (to avoid market saturation and competition)," according to historian Paul Hirt, citing a 1946 American Forestry Association report. It also involved developing shared fire-management goals, in response to on-the-ground conditions and the requirement for federal-state cooperation as outlined in the Clark-McNary Act (1924).[13]

These dynamics shifted and intensified in the 1970s and 1980s, for by then many of the checkerboard properties had been sold to timber companies. To service their accumulated debt, Champion International and Plum Creek, among other major operations, rapidly accelerated their timber harvests, which had a major impact on the Forest Service. Because the agency made "assumptions about the rate and style of management on these intermingled private lands," many of which proved inaccurate, it was confronted with "unexpected changes in environmental conditions" to which it was forced to respond. In the northern Rockies, for instance, the Clearwater, Kootenai, and Lolo national forests reduced their harvests as a consequence of heavier-than-anticipated logging on checkerboard lands; in 1991, faced with a range of severe environmental degradations resulting from clearcutting on private lands, Lolo Supervisor Orville Daniels went so far as to prohibit "cutting on 289,000 acres of its adjacent intermingled lands."[14]

Daniels' actions helped trigger a broader reappraisal among public-lands agencies and non-profit organizations about the difficulties of achieving landscape-scale analysis and management in a checkerboarded terrain. Since then, the goal has been to close the gaps in ownership and fill in the holes through land purchases and exchanges. This process has picked up in pace in reaction to timber companies disposing of their wooded assets, sales that have increased the environmental pressures on the national forests and national parks. In concert with NGOs such as the Trust for Public Land (TPL), the Forest Service has negotiated with corporations and other private landowners to purchase large, contiguous tracts. In 2003, for example, TPL, the Doris Duke Charitable Foundation, Gallatin National Forest, and Montana Senator Conrad Burns negotiated the purchase of upwards of 3,400 acres in the Taylor Fork drainage, which contains critical elk and grizzly-bear habitat northwest of Yellowstone National Park; more than a decade in the making, the complicated land purchase as part of the Forest Service's effort "to end the 'checkerboard' pattern of private land holdings that once dominated the west side of the Gallatin National Forest."[15]

The Taylor Fork purchase, and the combination of forces and funds it required, is an example of the recent "profusion of actors, and arrangements, and institutions" seeking more "collaborative, less confrontational ways to manage natural resources that span various institutional boundaries," which Sally Fairfax has dubbed the new "mosaic" of land management in the American west. It is also revelatory of the kind of proactive, wide-angled perspective that guided Orville Daniels's actions more than a decade earlier, and that should shape discussions within the Forest Service as it develops management policies in response to land fragmentation and private-lands development.[16]

The environmental implications of private-land development are straightforward. But there are also crucial political implications that will shape the context of future public-lands management. First among these is that national-forest management will become even more contested in the future because of intensifying development occurring on private lands. A compensation principle will become more evident. In other words, as private lands are developed and fragmented, relatively intact public lands will become increasingly valuable, and conservationists will want them further protected. Examples abound. The Forest Service, for instance, recognized the obvious in its 2001 roadless rule: "In an increasingly developed landscape, large unfragmented tracts of land become more important" (66 Fed. Reg. 3245). The ever-controversial Tongass National Forest provides another example, as it receives disproportionate public attention, and is thus the scene of considerable conflict because of the timber liquidation that has taken place on adjacent private native forests. Conservationists in southeast Alaska regularly ask the Forest Service to consider this interconnected landscape when making forest plans and project-level decisions, and are more likely to legally challenge the agency because of the relative difficulty of challenging private forestry practices.[17]

Second, it is reasonable to expect that National Environmental Policy Act's cumulative-impact requirement will be re-tested as a way to force the agency to analyze and adjust for what is happening at the "landscape level." Regulations define that requirement as an assessment of "the impact on the environment which results from the incremental impact of the action when added to other past, present, and reasonably foreseeable future actions regardless of what agency (Federal or non-Federal) or person undertakes such other actions ... [and] ... can result from individually minor but collectively significant actions taking place over a period of time" (40 C.F.R. §1508.7). This language increasingly is a focus of litigation, with the Forest Service most often sued in recent years. In cases heard by the Ninth Circuit Court of Appeals from 1995 to 2004, the agency lost nine of its thirteen. Though cumulative impact/effects case law is mixed, some courts have been reluctant to require agencies to seriously consider actions occurring on non federal lands and make corresponding adjustments. But such judicial deference to the Forest Service might change in the face of unprecedented fragmentation and the permanent loss of habitat, especially when development is so "reasonably foreseeable." And when viewed in conjunction with the strictures of the Endangered Species Act, National Forest Management Act, and other laws, this unwieldy provision could become even more important in the future.[18]

Third, it is reasonable to expect increased litigation by conservationists, who will challenge agency projects for not adequately considering private-land development and its impact on land, fish, wildlife, and water. Laws such as NEPA, the ESA, and the Clean Water Act, among others, will be invoked for this purpose. A parallel political campaign, emphasizing the public/private lands connection, is just as likely.

Finally, as the Forest Service itself has recognized, more citizen and user-group demands will be placed on the agency. Naturally, such demands will often be contradictory and disgruntled interests will challenge the agency when they fail to get what they want. The agency is used to this, of course, but the demands will become more pronounced in the future, from calls for increased access (partially due to fewer recreational opportunities on private lands) to more fire prevention and control.[19]

Calls to focus on private-land development may also come from unexpected quarters and force the agency to reconsider old problems in a new light. Take grazing-lease decisions, for instance, and the debate over "cows versus condos." Will the demise of public-lands ranching lead to further land fragmentation as ranchers sell and/or subdivide their adjacent private property? Debate notwithstanding, it is reasonable to ask the Forest Service to consider the environmental impacts of their leasing decisions at a landscape level, with possible threats to private land included.

The USFS has identified private-lands development as a critical problem, but what can be done about it? There are a few options the agency might employ. In the past it has employed a "policy toolbox" or "portfolio" to deal with development and intermixed ownership problems. Governmental regulation, land acquisition (e.g., Land and Water Conservation Fund), land exchanges, conservation easements (e.g., forest legacy program), private-land use planning and zoning, ecosystem management, habitat-conservation planning, tax- and incentive-based approaches, among other strategies and programs (e.g., state and private forestry), should be considered in this context. Forest Service leadership is also considering other options, such as the creation of markets and payments for ecosystem services, changes in rangeland policy that would help prevent ranchers from subdividing, and building partnerships with state and local governments. Instead of analyzing each tool's potential and limitations, here are a few additional opportunities, ideas, and questions that have not received as much attention.[20]

How, if at all, will the private-lands problem be addressed in the current forest-planning and decision-making process? To start at the apex of the pyramid, consider the Forest and Rangeland Renewable Resources Planning Act (RPA) of 1974. Its resource assessment provides a much-needed macro-level look at U.S. forest management, from timber and recreation inventories to trends in population growth and urban development. It is within this process, in fact, that the Forest Service has so clearly identified the open-space challenge.

The loss of open space is given some attention in the 2004 USFS Strategic Plan, but how far and fast that vision trickles down to the forest level is hard to discern. Furthermore, in this plan much less is said about how the agency intends to deal with this threat than others such as wildland fire and invasive species. Perhaps this is because of the problem's relative complexity or because the objectives and performance measures are harder to quantity and evaluate (compared to, say, acreage treated for hazardous fuels or invasives).

Further down the pyramid are forest plans. But under the 2005 and 2007 National Forest Management Act (NFMA) planning regulations, these non-decision documents are merely "strategic and aspirational" in nature and are categorically excluded from NEPA analysis.[21] So even if they addressed the private-land problem, it would be in the most cursory fashion. Most forest-plan revisions will not consider the issue. Take, for example, the Lolo and Flathead draft forest plan revisions, which do not analyze corporate timber divestment generally or how Plum Creek's particular real estate development plans may impact natural-resource management in the region.[22]

At the pyramid's base are project-level decisions, and it is at this level that the agency might respond to private-land development or where cumulative effects analysis will occur. Just as likely, however, is a more constricted view, with managers deeming the private-lands problem beyond a project's "purpose and need." And given the widespread use of categorical exclusions by the agency, at the project and plan level, it is debatable whether landscape-level analysis will prove the exception to the rule; a 2007 GAO Report indicates, for instance, that from 2003 to 2005, 72 percent of vegetation-management projects were approved using categorical exclusions.[23]

Planning regulations notwithstanding, the Forest Service might consider using more programmatic, regional, watershed, and/or place-based environmental impact statements in the future. In 1997, the Council on Environmental Quality recommended a place-based approach to decision making and NEPA-based strategic planning, partly as a more effective way to address cumulative effects within a particular geographic area. The CEQ-sponsored NEPA Task Force (2003) also recommended programmatic analyses and tiering as ways to reduce or eliminate redundant analyses and more efficiently address cumulative effects; it also found this type of analysis conducive to collaborative and adaptive-based approaches to planning, two current Forest Service priorities (70 Fed. Reg. 1023, Jan. 5, 2005). Collaboration will certainly be required in dealing with private-land development, leading the agency to seriously engage a number of actors, from counties to private-property owners. If this approach to planning is implemented, it must also provide a planning roadmap, letting the public know when deferred issues will be addressed and final decisions made.[24]

Another possible response is a type of "compensatory management," in which national forests are increasingly protected as private lands become fragmented. Conservationists will need to prioritize this argument, while drawing on various environmental laws to sustain their case—for example, grizzly-bear delisting in the greater Yellowstone area (and the resulting forest plan amendments) (70 Fed. Reg. 69,854, Nov. 17, 2005). The Natural Resources Defense Council advocates that private-land growth patterns correlate to adjacent public-land management. "Protection and restoration on public lands," in other words, "may need to increase to compensate for the loss of private land habitat due to development."[25]

Such compensation may already have been practiced, if only episodically: though not directly in response to private-land development, Forest Service timber-harvest levels have precipitously declined since the late 1980s in proportion to the rise in harvesting on private timberlands, so some type of compensatory balancing has occurred. But the forest-management wars are far from over. Future debates will be in terms of fire, access, motorized recreation, and over how to pay for forest health and restoration goals, among others, the resolution of which will require landscape-level analyses.[26]

Some sort of policy review, commission, or systematic analysis should also be considered as a way to proceed. Much like the last public-lands-law review commission in 1970, it could employ a comprehensive approach to analyze the problems and challenges of public-lands management within the context of land fragmentation and timberland divestment. However organized, the commission's purpose would be to assess the significant changes that have taken place in public-lands management in the U.S. since NFMA and ponder constructive policy responses. This sort of political re-evaluation and policy analysis might prove more helpful than dealing with such issues through science-driven cumulative-effects analysis or an RPA assessment that is designed to provide data, not policy options.

From their creation, the national forests have been impacted by actions taking place on private land, and agency leaders often have responded in some fashion, often by reducing harvests. There is historical precedent if the Forest Service chooses to play a leadership role in acting across boundaries. There are several ways that the agency could respond to the private-land development problem, from how it prioritizes its land-acquisition program to how it addresses the issue in the forest planning and NEPA process. If the agency adopts a more narrow perspective, without taking a landscape-level view and situating the management of the national forests in its larger context, we should expect a growing number of outside interests to challenge the agency using an assortment of laws to do so.

Notes

1. Dale Bosworth, "Sustaining America's forests: Challenges and opportunities," Sept. 18, 2006, speech to National Association of State Foresters, Anchorage, AK. Available online at http://www.fs.fed.us/news/2006/speeches.shtml; last accessed June 21, 2011.
2. R. J. Alig, A. J. Plantinga, S. Ahn, and J. D. Kline, *Land Use Changes Involving Forestry in the United States: 1952 to 1997, with projections to 2050.* USDA Forest Service General Technical Report, 2003. PNW-GTR-587.
3. USDA Forest Service, *Four threats to the health of the nation's forests and grasslands* (2007); http://www.fs.fed.us/projects/four-threats/; last visited Feb. 7, 2007.
4. Government Accountability Office, *Wildland fire management: Lack of a cohesive strategy hinders agencies' cost containment efforts,* 2007. GAO-07-427T.
5. USDA Forest Service, North Central Research Station, *Landscape Change Integrated Program,* 2007. http://www.ncrs.fs.fed.us/IntegratedPrograms/lc/; last visited Feb. 9, 2007.
6. Alig et al., *Land Use Changes Involving Forestry in the United States.*
7. USDA Forest Service, *Four threats to the health of the nation's forests and grasslands.*
8. N. E. Block, N.E. and V.A. Sample, *Industrial timberland divestitures and investments: opportunities and challenges in forestland conservation,* (Washington, DC: Pinchot Institute for Conservation, 2001); Jim Rinehart, "U. S. Timberland post-recession: Is it the same asset?" (April 2010), http://investmentforestry.com/resources/1%20-%20Post-Recession%20Timberland.PDF, last accessed December 19, 2011.
9. American Farmland Trust, "Strategic ranchland in the Rocky Mountain West," 2007. http://www.farmland.org/resources/rockymtn/default.asp; last accessed Feb. 14, 2007.
10. USDA Forest Service, *Four threats to the health of the nation's forests and grasslands;* USDA Forest Service, North Central Research Station, *Landscape Change Integrated Program;* USDA Forest Service, *2000 RPA Assessment of Forests and Grasslands,* 2001. FS-687: http://www.fs.fed.us/pl/rpa/publications_in_support_of_the_2.htm; last visited Feb. 7, 2007; P. H. Gobster, R. G. Haight, and D. Shriner, "Landscape change in the midwest: an integrated research and development program," *Journal of Forestry* 98(3), 2000: 9-14; D. J. Nowak and J. T. Walton, "Projected urban growth (2000-2050) and its estimated impact on the US forest resource," *Journal of Forestry,* 103(8), 2005: 383-89. D. J. Nowak, J.T. Walton, J.F. Dwyer, L.G. Kaya, and S. Myeong, "The increasing influence of urban environments on US forest management," *Journal of Forestry,* 103(8), 2005: 377-82.
11. Franklin B. Hough, *Report Upon Forestry* Vol. III (Washington, D.C.: Government Printing Office, 1882); Harold K. Steen, *The U. S. Forest Service: A History* (Durham, N.C.: Forest History Society, 2004).
12. Richmond L. Clow, "Timber Users, Timber Savers: The Homestake Mining Company and the First Regulated Timber Harvest," in Char Miller, ed., *American Forests: Nature, Culture, and Politics* (Lawrence: University Press of Kansas, 1997), p. 71-86; Gifford Pinchot, *Breaking New Ground* (Washington, D.C.: Island Press, 1998), p. 141; G. A. Gonzalez, *Corporate Power and the Environment: The Political Economy of U. S. Environmental Policy* (New York: Rowan & Littlefield Publishers, Inc., 2001).

13. Nancy Langston, *Forest Dreams, Forest Nightmares: The Paradox of Old Growth in the Inland West* (Seattle: University of Washington Press, 1995), p. 158-59; Paul W. Hirt, *A Conspiracy of Optimism: Management of the National Forests Since World War Two* (Lincoln: University of Nebraska Press, 1997), p. 54.

14. Hirt, *A Conspiracy of Optimism*, p. 276-77.

15. Trust for Public Land, "3400 Acres Near Yellowstone Protected": http://www.tpl. org/tier3_cd.cfm?content_item_id=12123&folder_id=678; Last visited August 30, 2007.

16. S. K. Fairfax, L. Gwin, M. A. King, L. Raymond, and L. A. Watt, *Buying Nature: The Limits of Land Acquisition as a Conservation Strategy, 1780-2004* (Cambridge, MA: MIT Press, 2005); S. K. Fairfax, H. Ingram, and L. Raymond, "Historical evolution and future of natural resources law and policy: the beginning of an argument and some modest predictions." Available at: http://www.colorado.edu/ law/centers/nrlc/summerconference/papers/Fairfax.Ingram.Raymond.Session1. HistoricalEvolution.pdf; last visited August 30, 2007.

17. Martin Nie, "Governing the Tongass: National Forest Conflict and Political Decision Making," *Environmental Law*, 2006 (36): 385-480; Kim Murphy, "Divergent interests at loggerheads in spectacular Tongass National Forest," *Los Angeles Times*, April 12, 2010: http://articles.latimes.com/2010/apr/12/nation/ la-na-tongass12-2010apr12; last accessed June 21, 2011; Kim Murphy, "Forest Service's new logging approach helps Alaska town," *Los Angeles Times*, April 9, 2011.

18. V. Alaric Sample, "Assessing cumulative environmental impacts: The case of national forest planning," *Environmental Law* 1991 (21): 839-61; M. D. Smith, "Cumulative impact assessment under the National Environmental Policy Act: An analysis of recent case law," *Environmental Practice*, 2006, 8(4): 228-40; L. Hartt, "*Pacific Coast Federation of Fishermen's Associations v. NMFS*: A case study on successes and failures in challenging logging activities with adverse cumulative effects on fish and wildlife," *Environmental Law*, 2002 (32): 671-716.

19. *USDA Forest Service strategic plan for fiscal years 2004-08*. FS-810; U.S. Forest Facts and Historical Trends. FS-696. Available at http://fia.fs.fed.us/library/ briefings-summaries-overviews/docs/ForestFactsMetric.pdf; last visited Oct. 5, 2007.

20. D. N. Bengston, J. O. Fletcher, and K. C. Nelson, "Public policies for managing urban growth and protecting open space: policy instruments and lessons learned in the United States," *Landscape and Urban Planning* 2004 (69): 271-86; C. Best and L. A. Wayburn, *America's Private Forests: Status and Stewardship* (Washington, D.C.: Island Press, 2001); H. Doremus, "A policy portfolio approach to biodiversity protection on private lands," *Environmental Science & Policy* 2003: 217-32; S. K. Fairfax, et al., *Buying Nature*; R. B. Keiter, "Biodiversity conservation and the intermixed ownership problem: from nature reserves to collaborative processes," *Idaho Law Review* 2005 (38):301-24; B. H. Thompson, "Providing biodiversity through policy diversity," *Idaho Law Review*, 2002 (38): 355-84; S. Collins, "The future of public land management," speech to Federal Lands Committee Meeting, National Cattlemen's Beef Association, Denver, CO: http://www.fs.fed.us/ news/2006/speeches.shtml; last accessed Feb. 14, 2007; Dale Bosworth, "Sustaining America's forests: Challenges and opportunities," Sept. 18, 2006: http://www.fs.fed.

us/news/2006/speeches.shtml; last accessed June 21, 2011; USDA Forest Service, 2006. Cooperating Across Boundaries: Partnerships to Conserve Open Space in Rural America: http://www.fs.fed.us/openspace/cooperatingacrossboundaries.pdf; last accessed Oct. 8, 2007.

21. See 70 Fed. Reg. 1023 (Jan. 5, 2005); 71 Fed. Reg. 75,481 (Dec. 15, 2006); 72 Fed. Reg. 48514 (Aug. 23, 2007).

22. USDA Forest Service, Proposed Land Management Plan: Bitterroot, Flathead, Lolo National Forests: http://www.fs.fed.us/r1/wmpz/documents/index.shtml; last accessed Feb. 14, 2007.

23. *Wildland fire management: Lack of a cohesive strategy hinders agencies' cost containment efforts.* GAO-07-427T.

24. *The National Environmental Policy Act: A Study of its Effectiveness After Twenty-Five Years* (Washington, D.C.: Council on Environmental Quality, 1997); *The NEPA Task Force Report to the Council on Environmental Quality: Modernizing NEPA Implementation* (2003).

25. L. Wilcox, *An Alternative Path to Grizzly Recovery in the Lower 48 States* (Washington, D.C.: Natural Resources Defense Council, 2004), 17.

26. U.S. Forest Facts and Historical Trends, FS-696: http://fia.fs.fed.us/library/briefings-summaries-overviews/docs/ForestFactsMetric.pdf; last visited Oct. 5, 2007.

The Once and Future Forest Service

The news from the Far North has not been good. In spring 2007, University of Alberta scientists reported that portions of the Canadian tundra were transforming into new forests of spruce and shrubs much more rapidly than once was imaginable. "The conventional thinking on treeline dynamics has been that advances are very slow because conditions are so harsh at these high latitudes and altitudes," reported Dr. Ryan Danby, a member of the UA research team. "But what our data indicate is that there was an upslope surge of trees in response to warmer temperatures. It's like [the forest] waited until conditions were just right, then it decided to get up and run, not just walk."[1]

The multifaceted impact of global climate change is chilling: as tundra converts to forest cover, species and their habitats must move higher up or die off; sheep and caribou are already responding to the environmental transformation that has affected members of Canada's First Nations dependent on these food sources. Moreover, the process feeds off itself: trees absorb more light than tundra and emit that energy as heat, further warming the atmosphere and reinforcing the very conditions that allow more spruce to flourish on the formerly treeless terrain. "These results are very relevant to the current debate surrounding climate change," Professor Danby noted, "because they provide real evidence that vegetation change will be quite considerable in response to future warming."[2]

The scientific data, and their myriad implications, raise key questions about how human institutions will respond to a human-generated crisis. This is particularly relevant to those land-management agencies, such as the U.S. Forest Service, that are responsible for innumerable bioregions and ecozones. How will the Forest Service steward its 193 million acres of forests and grasslands as the climate and landscape shift in relation to one another?[3]

That confounding question comes at a fascinating moment in the agency's history. Founded in 1905, in the immediate aftermath of its centennial celebrations the Forest Service found itself with a golden opportunity to consider whether its prior commitments will allow it to celebrate its *bi*centennial. That may seem an odd statement. After all, the Forest Service has managed to weather serious challenges in the past, a legacy suggesting it might prove as nimble when confronted with future trials, however unpredictable those global warming may pose. That said, the agency's history might not be a useful guide to a future layered with the dilemmas a warmer earth is expected to produce. However traumatic climate change may end up being, however disruptive its impact on the agency's previous patterns of behavior and action, analyzing the agency's past still may provide insight into its future actions. How will its leaders, line officers, rangers, and staff daily face complexities posed by an integrated series of forces that may overwhelm their capacity to manage landscapes? How will they respond to the welter of opportunities and challenges that already have emerged and will arise? These are not just policy questions but also have a historical dimension, for as Richard Neustadt and Ernest May observe: "seeing the past can help one envision alternative futures."[4]

This essay is concerned with identifying some of the alternative futures that the U. S. Forest Service might face, in particular three possible paths that could redefine its structure and mission. For the sake of clarity, I have segregated the three tracks but in reality they might well merge or intersect at various points in time, a speculative approach that is designed to provoke a larger discussion about land management in a changing climate.

SCENARIO ONE: EVOLUTIONARY DYNAMICS

The Forest Service has evolved in relation to the lands that it manages, establishing a dynamic interaction between the environment and the professional conservationists who seek to manage it, which confirms a broader claim: "History has repeatedly demonstrated that the health and welfare of human societies are fundamentally dependent on the health and welfare of their forests." This reciprocity, in its particularity and broad sweep, may prove the key to the agency's long-term survival. Because over time it has had to adapt to shifts in political temper, scientific knowledge, and social concern, its legacy of resilience also may define its twenty-first century behavior, enabling it to morph as required while retaining its core responsibilities and organizational structure.[5]

The Forest Service's creation depended on an argument about evolving landscapes. Three maps illustrating an article by William B. Greeley, the agency's third chief, make the case. Entitled "Virgin Forest Cover: 1620, 1850, 1920," they tell a story of profound environmental change as the original forest cover of what would become the United States was cut down, and hint at the Forest Service's mitigatory role. Early U. S. foresters believed that 1620 America was virginal so they could highlight the differences between those Euro-American settlers, farmers, and industrialists who slashed their way through ancient forests and latter-day Forest Service professionals, whose function was to protect and steward the remaining resources.

In political terms, the Forest Service produced such images to convince the nation that its work was critical to national security. To repair the land required an organization whose mission was to restore what had been destroyed. Replant, regenerate, repair: this would be the agency's environmental ethos for its first fifty years, from 1905 to 1945.

Yet embedded within that purpose was an intense anxiety, best captured in a 1908 cartoon: "Uncle Sam as He May Appear in Twenty Years." It depicts a crew-cut Uncle Sam—with stumps standing in as hair stubble—who like Samson has been shorn of his power, too weak to maintain his authority and expand his reach. Contemporaries understood that the U.S. was on the cusp of imperial dominance. By 1910, the American gross national product had exceeded the combined output of England, France, and Germany. Yet in recognizing that they had the chance to supplant Europe, many Americans were also haunted by the specter that they would miss this opportunity by acting as other empires had—by consuming and devastating their natural resources at such a clip and to such an extent that their economy would collapse along with their dreams of hegemonic power.[6]

Conservationists played a part in this wider cultural debate: their descriptions of forest devastation and the resultant "timber famine" dovetailed with their prescription—to create a system of public lands dedicated to the practice of conservative resource management. This argument had emerged in the aftermath of the publication of George Perkins Marsh's seminal work, *Man and Nature: Earth as Modified by Human Action* (1864), and gained momentum in the 1870s and 1880s as the American Forestry Association, fishing and hunting clubs, and women's groups agitated for regulatory mechanisms to control resource exploitation. Their agitation had an impact: in the 1870s the Division of Forestry was created within the Department of Agriculture. In 1891, Congress passed the Forest Reserve Act, granting the president power "from time to time, [to] set apart and reserve in any State or Territory having public land bearing forests ... public reservation." Within a year, President Benjamin Harrison had set aside more than thirteen million acres as forest reserves, and his successor, Grover Cleveland, added another five million; by 1899, the number had swelled to forty million. But it was not until 1897 that administrative control over these reserves was codified.[7]

President Theodore Roosevelt helped tip the balance in favor of conservation. Between 1901 and 1908, he added 110 million acres to the National Forest System; he also signed off on the transfer of these lands from Interior to Agriculture and created the Forest Service. In short order, the agency's first chief, Gifford Pinchot, began training rangers to survey and map the lands within the boundaries of the new national forests; pressed for the resolution of legal challenges, which ultimately led to Supreme Court decisions affirming the Forest Service's statutory standing and authority to manage the forests and grasslands; and lobbied Congress for budget increases to match its expanded duties.

With the establishment of these boundaries—topographical, political, and legal—the Forest Service went to work on its central managerial task from 1905 until World War Two, the regeneration of battered terrain in the west; during the Great Depression its charge widened to include gullied southern farmlands and the Dust-Bowl plains. By World War Two, the Forest Service's engagement had proved national in scope and local in significance; it had become the nation's soft-hatted custodial agent.[8]

That hat hardened with the advent of global war and postwar prosperity. Then its task was to get out the cut. In 1940, two billion board feet were harvested on the national forests; by 1960 the figure had zoomed upward, topping out at twelve billion board feet in the late 1980s. This shift was of incalculable importance and is perhaps best reflected in the controversies that erupted in the 1970s over clearcutting on Montana's Bitterroot National Forest and West Virginia's Monongahela National Forest. For its supporters, clearcutting signaled the agency's newfound ability to harvest trees in once-difficult terrain and its laudable ambition to turn natural forests into plantations. For its critics, this was a dire reflection of the Forest Service's technological fixation. So intense did the debate become that even an internal task force chided agency employees on the Bitterroot for acting as if "resource production goals come first and … land management considerations take second place."[9]

Protests over clearcutting and the technological imperative provoked a backlash against the Forest Service, sparking federal lawsuits, local demonstrations, and a welter of state and congressional inquiries. When the dust had settled, a new legal environment had emerged. Among its most critical components was the 1976 National Forest Management Act (NFMA), which gave the public a much stronger role in determining forest planning and set strict limits on the Forest Service's clearcutting practices.

The NFMA was the last in a remarkable series of landmark environmental initiatives. Beginning with the 1964 Wilderness Act, and including the Wild and Scenic Rivers Act (1968), National Environmental Policy Act (1970), the various Clean Air and Clean Water Act amendments of the 1970s, and Endangered Species Act (1973), these bills constitute the second great wave of environmental activism. The end result has been that these initiatives regulate the very land-management regulatory agencies, such as the Forest Service and the National Park Service, that were born during the first surge of environmental legislation, crafted in the Progressive Era.

Since these laws' adoption, the agency has appeared to be wandering in the forest. Pounded in federal court, faced with drastic budget cuts and sharp reductions in personnel, it has struggled to find its way, leading one former chief to argue it is mired in "analysis paralysis" that is preventing it from doing its proper work. Complicating this struggle to define its contemporary mission have been steep declines in timber harvests, escalating population pressures along the urban-wildland interface, increased recreational use, intensifying forest fires, and serious water-management issues. No wonder the agency's morale is low.[10]

The Forest Service's initiatives reflect this sometimes-shaky sense of self and its wavering commitments (real and perceived) are linked to the larger culture's curious inability to embody the environmental principles it purports to embrace. One example should suffice: through legal pressure and political compromise, the public has forced the Forest Service to scale back its timber harvests, from twelve billion board feet in the late 1980s to 2.44 billion in 2011. Yet American demand for wood products has increased every year for the past fifty. We have accomplished this by a simple expedient—outsourcing demand to Canada, Eastern Europe, southern Africa, and the equatorial band of tropical rainforests, thus exporting our environmental problems to other, often poorer, parts of the planet.[11]

Such myopia only roils the political context in which the Forest Service operates, hindering the agency's ability to revise its land-management practices on the national forests.

Still, a persuasive case can be made that what has appeared to be a lack of coherent guidelines may simply be a necessary byproduct of evolutionary change. It is tricky to decipher, in the midst of a transition, the precise nature *of* that transition. The agency's history supports this view. Its management of resources, the emphasis of which has moved from grass to trees to water, has revealed its ability, however constrained, to shift its ground, to adapt to changes in politics and polity, ideas and images. This is how all organisms survive.

SCENARIO TWO: DEVOLUTIONARY PROGRESS

Yet there are times when the rate of change is so radical that organisms emerge as something else altogether. Indeed, a proposed alteration that the Forest Service has faced—and to date has fended off—is the devolution of its lands and authority to the individual states in which its forests and grasslands are located. Those who have argued for this outcome have drawn on a powerful strain in American political thought, with the Tenth Amendment as their prooftext: "The powers not delegated to the United States by the Constitution, nor prohibited by it to the States, are reserved for the States respectively, or to the people." In attempting to define the precise relationship between federal and state sovereignty, a central issue in the United States since the eighteenth century, the amendment actually makes clear that this relationship is in considerable tension. The Forest Service knows this full well, for the agency long has been a flashpoint in the heated political debate between states rights and national prerogatives.

With reason: in the early twentieth century western critics of President Theodore Roosevelt alleged that his creation of the Forest Service and the national forests were but a means to expand presidential authority. That is why they erupted in anger when he withdrew 110 million acres from the public domain during his two administrations, sparking the first Sagebrush Rebellion, which simmered between 1905 and 1908. Although the Supreme Court legitimized the agency's managerial control of these lands (and thus implicitly supported Roosevelt's actions) through a series of test cases resolved in 1911, its decisions did not defuse western resentment. In the 1950s, western livestock interests reignited the debate but without success. No more successful was the 1990s "Wise Use" movement, which demanded that the federal government relinquish its rights to the national forests. In this overheated environment, Pinchot, mocked in a 1908 cartoon that was entitled "Czar Pinchot and his Cossack Rangers," would have felt right at home.[12]

Although this version of the states-rights argument has never gained much traction in the United States, it did in Canada and New Zealand, and an analysis of these other countries' experiences helps sets American land-management politics in an international context. Originally, Canada and New Zealand had followed a similar path to that of the United States:

in a federalized structure in which national and provincial governments maintained different levels of sovereignty, each country established a national forest system under the management of a professional forest service. Like the U.S. Forest Service, the Canadian and New Zealand agencies were expected to oversee and maintain their valuable resource base. That expectation is not surprising. Gifford Pinchot had been a strong proponent of the Canadian conservation movement, and all three societies had adapted European ideas for how to regulate resource exploitation. Linked at their creation, it would have been reasonable to suppose that the futures of these three professional agencies also would have run in tandem.

That is not what happened. Founded in 1899, the Canadian Forest Service developed simultaneously with schools of forestry. (The first of these, at the University of Toronto, was directed by German-born forester Bernhard Fernow, who had recently resigned as head of the U.S. Division of Forestry.) These schools' graduates joined the new agency's staff, and their scientific expertise shaped the organization's managerial perspective; by 1924, Canadian foresters had 9.2 million acres under management. But within six years, this short-lived experiment in federal forestry was over. In 1930, as the depression bore down, all national forest lands were returned to the provinces from which originally they had been appropriated, and the agency's budget and staff were cut drastically. The concept of a national agency with land-management regulatory control never recovered. Over the years, the Canadian Forest Service's bureaucratic status has been downgraded from an agency to a department, from a service to a division; it regained its departmental status in 1989 but a decade earlier had lost a critical part of its research responsibilities when its forest products laboratories were privatized. Because it no longer has a land base or a scientific mission, the Canadian Forest Service now serves as a "navigator" for private and provincial foresters and forests. Its mission statement reflects this change in function: "The Canadian Forest Service promotes the sustainable development of Canada's forests and the competitiveness of the Canadian forest sector." Not all have been happy with its new role as a promoter or catalyst. As Ken Druska and Bob Burt have observed, at "various points in its history, some of its leaders or its critics have looked wistfully at its southern counterpart, the U.S. Forest Service, with its vast national forest base, and its authoritative position in U.S. society."[13]

New Zealand showed no such wistfulness when in the 1980s it embarked on an even more rapid devolution of its public forests. The nation's central role in forestry had begun seven decades earlier. In 1913, after nearly a century of largely unregulated and intense harvesting of native forests, a Royal Commission on Forestry was appointed to evaluate forest conditions, determine which lands would remain in pubic control, define their purposes, and estimate future demand for timber and other resources. The commission concluded that New Zealand needed a commissioner of forestry and a professional forest service that would manage the state-owned woods. Although World War One delayed the implementation of these recommendations, by 1920 they were enacted, new schools of forestry were established, and management commenced. Sixty years later, the national government owned more than 50 percent of New Zealand's commercial forests and it dominated the national timber economy.

By 2000, that was no longer true: the government owned only 6 percent of commercial forestland; 34 percent was held by Maori trusts, 3 percent was under local control; the largest ownership group was international timber companies. Corporate, for-profit forestry now was the law of the land.

Why and how had this rapid transition occurred? In 1986, the Labor government, responding to the country's sluggish economy, first corporatized, then privatized the resource agencies. One year later, the New Zealand Forest Service was abolished and folded into a new Department of Conservation. The new Ministry of Forestry was, like its Canadian peer, to serve as a policy shop, and the New Zealand Forestry Corporation, gained control of the state's commercial forestry operations on 4.4 million hectares (almost eleven million acres), focusing on market-driven resource management and the creation of a profitable forest sector.[14]

Neither the Canadian nor the New Zealand model has been seriously advocated in the United States. True, those who would like to reduce or eliminate the U.S. Forest Service's regulatory clout have proposed transferring the national forests to the states. But this proposal does not resemble the Canadian experience of returning lands to the provinces; the U.S. national forests had always been federal property. Nor is it clear that the various states in which national forests are sited would welcome a complete dismantling of the federal presence; they might not have the budgets, staff, or political will to maintain these invaluable lands.[15]

Much more plausible are calls for the creation of a cooperative conservation strategy in which local groups and federal land managers together develop forest plans. This has a historical basis, too: Circular 21

(1898), which promoted the agency's cooperation with private landowners, found its analogue in other initiatives that encouraged forest rangers to discuss with local communities and economic interests how best to manage the forests. More recently, cooperative actions have been nurtured by the National Forest Management Act and the Endangered Species Act that require public participation and interagency coordination; they have also been energized by community environmental initiatives promoted at the 1997 Seventh American Forest Congress. Bolstered by university-sponsored think tanks, such as the Public Policy Research Institute at the University of Montana, they have launched several successful ventures, including the Quincy Library Group (1992) and the New Ranch program developed by the Quivira Coalition (1997); the latter seeks to operate within what it calls the "radical center—a neutral place where people could explore their interests instead of argue their positions—and at the grassroots, literally the 'grass' and the 'roots,' where we believed, trust needed to be built anew."[16]

The "Lubrecht Conversations," held outside of Missoula, Montana, in 1998 shared this commitment to a "bottom up" approach to national-policy reform. Local-consensus management would evolve to include wider watershed and bioregional perspectives that then would shape the national agenda. Most captivating was the group's call for the creation of a "virtual" Region 7 within the Forest Service wherein districts and forests would propose "to develop practical collaborative decision-making processes at the local/regional level, which might eventually evolve into a national restatement of basic mission." If acceptable, the Forest Service would fund the experiment but would not retain authority over its design or implementation.[17]

Although to date "Region 7" remains but a tantalizing idea, other experimental formats have been enacted. One of these is the Valles Caldera Trust (2000), a government-owned entity that provides management and administrative services for the Valles Caldera National Preserve in northern New Mexico. This national preserve suggests the array of options that have been emerging in timber towns and ranch country in response to decades of political discord, legal wrangling, and bureaucratic entanglement. This development received another push in August 2005, when the White House Conference on Cooperative Conservation convened, a sign that community-oriented, collaborative conservation has captured considerable political interest and generated significant momentum.[18]

Whether this top-down support of grassroots actions will be manifest in long-term reform is uncertain. But these projects' incremental development, innovative perspectives, and experimental character give them a much greater chance of success in revising the reigning principles of public land management in the United States than anything advocated by the Wise Use movement or modeled in the devolutionary actions of Canada and New Zealand.[19]

SCENARIO THREE: REVOLUTIONARY IMPULSE

The creation of a new Department of Conservation in the executive branch, by contrast, would expand the federal managerial presence and its regulatory authority. With a seat in the cabinet, this department would house the nation's most important land management agencies—the Bureau of Land Management, Bureau of Reclamation, Fish and Wildlife Service, Forest Service, Geological Survey, National Resources Conservation Service, National Park Service, among other entities. By creating economies of scale and greater efficiencies of action, this new department would save money and would serve as a standard bearer for the modern environmental movement.

Such an approach flies in the face of contemporary environmentalism, which stresses local agency over national solutions; and so would not sit easily with Republican Party ideologies, either. Yet an unreflective dismissal of this possibility may lead conservationists to miss a chance to restructure federal land-management institutions and their delivery of environmental services. It may turn out that the most effective way to secure much-desired bottom-up reform is through simultaneous top-down change.

That said, none of the previous efforts to establish a Department of Conservation has been successful. When the Forest Service was created in 1905, it, like its progenitor, the Bureau of Forestry, was located in the Department of Agriculture. The nation's forests, however, were administered in Interior. To bring the foresters and the forests together, Gifford Pinchot faced two choices: shift his tiny staff to Interior to be united there with the national forest reserves, or seek the transfer of millions of forested acres from one cabinet department to another. Because he was convinced that Interior's history of corruption would compromise the newly formed Forest Service, he chose the latter path. Seven years after he inaugurated discussions in 1898, Congress and Interior signed off on the transfer.

The Department of Interior has been trying to recover these lost acres ever since. In the 1920s, Interior Secretary Albert Fall pushed for the transfer of the Forest Service and its forests but failed. Ten years later, Franklin D. Roosevelt's secretary of Interior, Harold Ickes, proposed a Department of Conservation as part of a broader New Deal scheme to reorganize the executive branch. His bid revolved around moving the Forest Service and national forests to Interior and pulling in other federal land-management agencies under one roof; this restructuring, he believed, would enable those who worked on soils to talk with those who worked with trees; hydrologists with botanists. In trying to finesse turf wars, Ickes ignited a contentious political brawl that damaged the Roosevelt administration.[20]

In anticipation of such potential problems, President Roosevelt had informed Secretary of Agriculture Harry A. Wallace in 1933–34 that he must not publicly protest or privately fight the Forest Service's impending transfer; Roosevelt also required Wallace to gag Ferdinand Silcox, chief of the Forest Service. Through back channels, Silcox asked sixty-eight-year-old Gifford Pinchot to come to the agency's aid, a request Pinchot gladly accepted, and his strategy was simple: if he whipped up a loud-enough storm of protest, he might force the president to recalibrate the costs associated with Ickes's concept. By the late 1930s, Pinchot had forced Roosevelt to capitulate.

This climatic struggle obscured a larger question about the best way to organize the management of the public lands. Would Ickes's vision of an integrated Department of Conservation have provided a more comprehensive leadership for and efficient stewardship of the nation's forests, rivers, and grasslands? We will never know, but the alluring idea of a unified conservation department has continued to attract adherents. In the early 1970s, the Nixon administration, at the same time it advocated the creation of the Environmental Protection Agency, pushed for the establishment of a Department of Natural Resources that would have been merged with Interior. The idea failed in part because Russell Train, head of the Environmental Protection Agency, argued against it. "There was some logic [to the idea,]" he recalled in 2006, "but I testified against it, against building a bigger bureaucracy. I was opposed to burying environmental responsibility in a big conglomeration with everything from Indian affairs to reclamation. The environment would have been submerged."[21]

Undaunted, President Jimmy Carter also floated the idea of a Department of Natural Resources in concert with his plan to create a Department of Energy; each would absorb disparate agencies and offer a more cost-effective and integrated management. Energy became a cabinet-level position in 1977, but Natural Resources did not get beyond the discussion stage. President Reagan proposed major land swaps between the Forest Service and the Bureau of Land Management, to streamline management (but not to merge the two agencies); the idea of a broader transfer resurfaced in the Clinton era and was re-floated during President Obama's first term. To date, nothing has come of these most recent discussions.[22]

Despite these various presidents' failure to create a conservation superagency, there are signs that at least a low level of integration of agency function is underway. In 1997, Congress authorized a program called Service First: Working Together, in which the Forest Service and the Bureau of Land Management were authorized to merge various functions. One such joint venture is the Durango Public Lands Center, through which the two agencies manage their lands in southwestern Colorado. The leadership of the San Juan National Forest and the San Juan Field BLM Office, like the twelve-person staff, are "cross delegated." Because each employee is responsible for "all aspects of the two agencies' work and is equally responsible to the USFS Regional Forester and BLM State Director," because each is required to be fluent in both agencies' statutory regulations and wears the two uniforms, this is an innovative, even unusual, arrangement. The San Juan is "the only organization in the country with a single team providing leadership in all aspects of land management and public service for the two federal agencies."[23]

These low-level interchanges are part of a larger attempt to merge scarce skills and resources among the nation's land-management agencies. More should be done, forest policy expert Sally K. Fairfax has argued, to facilitate the convergence of these agencies' identities and missions. Noting that "The historic distinctions and feuds" between the Forest Service, National Park Service, and Bureau of Land Management "no longer matter," she observes:

> The hostility between the advocates of forest reserves and park reserves that began before either agency was formed conceals the fact that for most of their existence, they have been more alike than not. As timber fades as a Forest Service preoccupation, and recreation emerges as dominant present and future concerns, the justifications for having multiple and distinct federal management agencies fade as well.[24]

Lending further credence to her argument is a November 2006 Memorandum of Understanding that the Bureau of Land Management and the Forest Service signed in partnership with the Fish and Wildlife Service and the National Park Service; it committed the four agencies "to carry out shared or joint management activities to achieve mutually beneficial resource management goals." This Service First authority has been utilized primarily for merging offices, issuing joint permits, sharing management, and creating single points of contact for resource programs. Given the patchwork of lands each agency manages and the proximity of their holdings, this integrative approach makes considerable sense, so much so that the Bureau of Indian Affairs, Bureau of Reclamation, and Army Corps of Engineers have been considering seeking Service First authorization. By this incremental fashion the dream of a Department of Conservation that has eluded several presidents and innumerable policy analysts might be fulfilled.[25]

FUTURE FOCUS

Separately, none of the three scenarios sketched out here—evolution, devolution, revolution—will have much chance of redefining the Forest Service's twenty-first-century structure or its guiding perspectives. None of these possibilities will be achieved without reference to and/or in combination with the others. Moreover, although any change in the agency's land-management mission will require internal support from the Forest Service's leadership and staff, the real locus of any such transformation lies in Congress and the executive branch. That is what Roger Sedjo, Senior Fellow at Resources for the Future, had in mind when he noted in 2000 that the Forest Service "no longer controls national forest policy. Instead, mandatory provisions of the law and regulations ... mean that the regional and local landscapes, watersheds, and their resources are now the focus of attention." Because the assessments of these resources' viability shape policy, the Forest Service and other public-land management agencies now "lack the institutional capacity and authority to fully develop and implement ecosystem conservation agendas and resource management programs." That these organizations lack the necessary clout is tied to their inability "to interpret and respond effectively to the public's priorities regarding national forest management."[26]

    To regain the capacity to listen to the citizenry and address its varied concerns, the Forest Service need only recall Gifford Pinchot's formative conviction that democratic debate was essential to determining the nature of public-lands management. He knew that the collaborative process of defining and achieving conservation stewardship on the national forests would never be easy but was convinced this process was the only way to safeguard these precious assets, a matter of even more pressing obligation in this vexing climate of change.

Notes

1. *Science Daily*, March 7, 2007, http://www.sciencedaily.com/releases/2007/03/070305140830.htm, accessed June 12, 2007.
2. *Ibid.*
3. Robert W. Malmsheimer, et al., "Forest Management Solutions for Mitigating Climate Change in the United States," special issue, *Journal of Forestry*, April/May 2008, p. 129-31.
4. Richard E. Neustadt and Ernest R. May, *Thinking in Time: The Uses of History for Decision-Makers*" (New York: Free Press, 1986), p. xv.
5. Tom Thompson, "Forestry and Climate Change," *Journal of Forestry*, April/May 2008, p. 113.
6. George Perkins Marsh, *Man and Nature: Earth as Modified by Human Action* (New York: C. Scribner, 1864); Gifford Pinchot, *The Fight for Conservation* (New York: Doubleday, Page & Co., 1910).
7. Marsh, *Man and Nature*; Harold K. Steen, *The U. S. Forest Service: A History* (Seattle: University of Washington Press, 1976); John Reiger, *American Sportsmen and the Origins of Conservation*, fourth edition (Corvallis: Oregon State University Press, 2001).
8. Char Miller, "Crisis Management: Challenge and Controversy in Forest Service History," *Rangelands*, June 2005, p. 14-18.
9. Martin Nie, "The Bitterroot Controversy," http://forestryencyclopedia.jot.com/WikiHome/Bitterroot%20Controversy, accessed June 12, 2007.
10. Jack Ward Thomas, "What Now? From a Former Forest Service Chief," in Roger Sedjo, ed., *A Vision for the Forest Service: Goals for Its Next Century* (Washington, D.C.: Resources for the Future, 2000), pp. 10–43; Char Miller, "Identity Crisis," *Forest Magazine*, Winter 2008, p. 44-47.
11. Michael P. Dombeck, Christopher A. Wood, and Jack E. Williams, *From Conquest to Conservation: Our Public Lands Legacy* (Washington, D.C.: Island Press, 2003).
12. William L. Graf, *Wilderness Preservation and the Sagebrush Rebellions* (Savage, MD: Rowman & Littlefield Publishers, 1990); Char Miller, *Gifford Pinchot and the Making of Modern Environmentalism* (Washington, D. C.: Island Pres, 2001), p. 163-67.
13. Mark Kuhberg, *One Hundred Rings and Counting: Forestry Education and Forestry in Toronto and Canada*, (Toronto: University of Toronto Press, 2009); Ken Druska and Bob Burt, "The Canadian Forest Service: Catalyst for the Forest Sector," *Forest History Today*, Spring/Fall 2001, p. 28.
14. Differing opinions about the meaning of this transformation may be found in Andrew D. McEwen, "Exit of State From Plantation Forest Ownership in New Zealand," http://www.maf.govt.nz/mafnet/unff-planted-forestry-meeting/conference-papers/exit-of-state-from-plantations.htm, accessed June 13, 2007; and Nicole Spence, "The Privatization of New Zealand Forests," *Journal of Forestry Research*, 2, 1997, pp. 203–6; for a discussion of some of the earlier history, see Michael M. Roche, "Reactions to Scarcity: The Management of Forest Resources in Nineteenth-Century Canterbury, New Zealand," *Journal of Forest History*, April 1984, pp. 82-91.
15. A domestic model for state-level control of public lands that has generated considerable interest is the 135 million acres of state-trust lands that have had

some economic success for some states; Jon Souter and Sally Fairfax, *State Trust Lands: History, Management, and Sustainable Use* (Lawrence: University Press of Kansas, 1996, and Sally Fairfax, "State Trust Lands Management: A Promising New Application for the Forest Service?" in Sedjo, ed., *A Vision for the Forest Service*, pp. 105–41, suggest that these trusts are an "appealing organizational option" to current federal land agencies.

16. For Quincy Library Group, see http://www.qlg.org/pub/contents/chron.htm; for Quivira, see http://quiviracoalition.org/About_Us/index.html; last accessed June 14, 2007; Martin Nie and Char Miller, "National Forest Management and Private Land Development: Historical, Political, and Planning Considerations," *Society and Natural Resources*,23:7, July 2010, p. 669-78; David A. Clary, *Timber and the Forest Service* (Lawrence: University Press of Kansas, 1986).

17. Region 7, which covered many eastern states, was eliminated in the 1960s from the Forest Service's organization structure; *The Legal Framework for Cooperative Conservation*, Collaborative Governance Report 1 (Missoula: Public Policy Research Institute, University of Montana, 2006), which is an outgrowth of the 2005 White House Conference on Cooperative Conservation, summarizes the federal legislative support for collaborative forestry; Elizabeth Beaver et al., "Seeing the Forest Service for the Trees: A Survey of Proposals for Changing National Forest Policy," Natural Resources Law Center, University of Colorado School of Law, June 25, pp. 27–29, http://www.colorado.edu/law/centers/nrlc/publications/Forestry_Reforms_Report.pdf, accessed June 14, 2007.

18. On the Valles Caldera National Preserve, see http://www.vallescaldera.gov/about/, accessed June 14, 2007; in June 2009, New Mexico's two senators, Jeff Binghaman and Tom Udall announced their support for turning the preserve over to the National Park Service, stripping it of its innovative public-private partnership: see http://vallescaldera.com/archives/1341, last accessed June 21, 2011.

19. Mexico's experiences with locally determined, collaborative forestry has caught the attention of the U.S. Forest Service, whose leadership has routinely attended workshops in Oaxaca; for background on and evaluations of the Mexican experience, see the special issue of *Journal of Sustainable Forestry*, 15:1, 2002, "Community-Based Approaches to Forest Management."

20. Char Miller, "Crisis Management: Challenge and Controversy in Forest Service History," *Rangelands*, June 2005, p. 14-18.

21. "Q&A: Russell Train, Green Legislator Pioneer," *American Forests*, Autumn 2006, p. 39.

22. In March 2008, Congress requested that GAO undertake a study of the feasibility of transferring the Forest Service to Interior; Christopher Lee, "Forest Service May Move to Interior," *Washington Post*, March 26, 2008, p. A3; see also, Ross W. Gorte, "Proposals to Merge the Forest Service and the Bureau of Land Management: Issues and Approaches," *Congressional Research Service Report for Congress*, May 5, 2008.

23. Information concerning the Durango Public Lands Center can be retrieved at http://www.co.blm.gov/sjra/ and http://www.fs.fed.us/r2/sanjuan/about/organization/servicefirst.pdf, accessed June 15, 2007.

24. Sally K. Fairfax, "When an Agency Outlasts Its Time: A Reflection," *Journal of Forestry*, July/August 2005, p. 265.